THEORY *of* REALITY

THEORY *of* REALITY

Evidence for Existence Beyond the Brain and Tools for Your Journey

DAVID O. WIEBERS, M.D.

Threshold World Press
Seattle, WA

Threshold World Press
Seattle, WA

Copyright © 2012 by David O. Wiebers, M.D.

All rights reserved. This book may not be reproduced in whole or in part, stored in a retrieval system, or transmitted in any form or by any means—electronic, mechanical, or other—without written permission from the author, except by a reviewer, who may quote brief passages in a review.

This book is written as a source of information only. The information contained in this book should by no means be considered a substitute for the advice, decisions or judgment of the reader's physician or other professional advisor. No decisions regarding diagnosis, prognosis or treatment should be made on the basis of this book alone.

All efforts have been made to ensure the accuracy of the information contained in this book as of the date of publication. The author and the publisher expressly disclaim responsibility for any adverse effects from the use or application of the information contained herein.

Illustrations by Jeffrey B. Nisley
Cover image courtesy of NASA
Text and cover design by Mary Ann Casler, Word Design & Publishing Services

Library of Congress Control Number: 2012945135

First printing, September 2012
Hardcover ISBN 978-0-9859375-2-2
Ebook ISBN 978-0-9859375-0-8

Printed in the USA on 100% postconsumer-waste recycled paper

10 9 8 7 6 5 4 3 2 1

CONTENTS

PREFACE ix

EDITORIAL NOTE xiii

THEORY OF REALITY OVERVIEW 1

THEORY OF REALITY CONDENSED MESSAGES 3

THEORY OF REALITY FUNDAMENTAL DESCRIPTION 7

THEORY OF REALITY CONSCIOUSNESS PARADIGM 15

ABOUT THE TOR KEY EVIDENCE CATEGORIES 21

KEY EVIDENCE CATEGORIES 23

A. THEORY OF REALITY PRIMARY EVIDENCE 25

1. *Evidence that Near-Death Experiences Are Valid, Real Phenomena and Not Hallucinations, Seizures or Some Other Aberration* — 25

2. *Evidence for Our Ability to Exist and Function Separately Without the Brain* — 37

3. *Evidence That Brain Activity in and of Itself Cannot Account for Consciousness* — 41

B. THEORY OF REALITY SECONDARY EVIDENCE 45

1. *Evidence for Intelligence Outside the Human Brain— Down to the Electron, Photon and C Unit Levels* — 45

2. *Evidence for Coherence and Resonance as Underlying Mechanisms for Communication at Multiple Levels* — 51

3. *Evidence for a Holographic Type of Organization Underlying Our Brains and Our Universe* — 57

4. *Evidence for a C Field as a Basic Underlying Matrix or Fabric for Reality (as We Experience It Here and in Other Dimensions) and for Some Unit of This (C Unit) as the Most Fundamental Building Block of the Universe* — 69

5. *Evidence for Various Types of Peak Experiences and Other Related Phenomena Being Associated with Discoveries, Creativity, and Other Types of Uncommon Insight and Understanding* — 77

6. Evidence for Other "Finer" Levels of Existence Enfolded into the Same Space and Time as This Physical Plane   83

7. Evidence for Particle and Wave Aspects of Subatomic Structures (as Documented by Physicists) and for How These Components Parallel the Particle and Wave Aspects of Consciousness, Energy and Matter   89

8. Evidence That "Empty Space" Is Not at All Empty and That It Instead Contains an Incredibly Vast Amount of Energy and Provides Insight into What is Hidden from Our Materialistic Senses and a Materialistic Conceptualization of the Universe   97

ANATOMY OF A SPIRITUAL ADVENTURE 103

TOOLS AND TECHNIQUES 111

1. Peak Experiences (PEs)   111
2. Near-Death Experiences (NDEs)   113
3. Out-of-Body Experiences (OOBEs)   119
4. Connecting with One's Higher Self (CWOHS)   129
5. After-Death Contact (ADC)   133
6. Past-Life Recall/Regression (PLR)   137
7. Other Tools and Techniques—Meditation, Yoga, Lucid Dreams/Dream Control, Visualization, Hypnosis, Contemplation/Prayer, Triggers/Facilitators   143
8. Enhancing Coherence, Resilience and Equanimity in One's Day-to-Day Life—Twelve Key Factors   147
   a. Develop a Balanced Worldview and Productive Attitude   149
   b. Develop an Internal Locus of Control   149

c. Approach Life with Gratitude, Generosity
   and Compassion ... 150
d. Cultivate Optimism ... 151
e. Know When to be Assertive ... 152
f. Increase the Amount of Laughter in Your Life ... 153
g. Involve Yourself in Music, the Arts and
   Other Forms of Creativity ... 154
h. Enhance Your Experiences of Love, Intimacy and
   Close Friendships ... 155
i. Get in Touch with Your Spiritual Side
   (Your Deeper Self) ... 157
j. Develop Your Optimal Program of Physical Exercise ... 158
k. Choose Brain-Healthy Nutrition ... 160
l. Maintain Optimal Sleep Habits ... 163

GLOSSARY OF ABBREVIATIONS 167

TOR EVIDENCE CATEGORY REFERENCES 169

TOR TOOLS AND TECHNIQUES REFERENCES 177

INDEX 181

ABOUT THE AUTHOR 195

ABOUT TOR GROUP 197

ABOUT TOR FOUNDATION 199

PREFACE

For as long as I can remember, I've been fascinated by the issues that underlie the Theory of Reality. My early training and subsequent work in the fields of medicine and neuroscience provided wonderful opportunities to learn from colleagues, patients and students and to experience the brain and consciousness from numerous perspectives in a variety of clinical and research settings. Even earlier, in my college days, I had taken a road less traveled to medical school by concentrating my coursework in physics, chemistry and mathematics, subjects which were not only fascinating, but which also provided very different ways to approach and reflect upon reality and the universe.

During my subsequent career as a neurologist and neuroscientist, with no particular need for prodding, I found myself consistently gravitating not only to the Science and Medical sections of bookstores but also to the Metaphysical, New Age, Self-Help and Spiritual sections of such stores in search of answers to many of the ongoing mysteries of science and to many of life's most profound and perplexing questions.

The last 40 years have brought with them an extraordinary evolution in our knowledge base in medicine, neuroscience and the physical sciences. During this time period, we have also witnessed a growing number of profound observational and experimental findings that our current scientific paradigms have no way to address or explain. Many of these findings come from medicine, neuroscience and the physical sciences themselves, and others emanate from what has traditionally been classified as metaphysical science.

Important and pioneering work has come from many diverse channels, and the findings and results have, in many cases, become recognized, verified and intuitively accepted throughout wide swaths of the general public. We have now come to a point where limiting ourselves to current scientific paradigms in the face of so much new evidence that does not fit with them would ultimately threaten the credibility of science and its applicability to the reality that we are collectively experiencing.

Over the years and decades, I have marveled at the brilliance and persistence of the diverse group of pioneers who have brought so many of these observational and experimental findings to light, and I have come to feel a great sense of indebtedness to them. I have been awed by what seemed to be a fairly consistent stream of important contributions emanating from different places and different approaches, and I have found myself in constant search of ways to decipher the critical elements of these findings and put some or all of the bits and pieces together to arrive at a greater and more profound appreciation or vision of the whole.

Ultimately, a number of important overarching concepts began to present themselves, and many of these concepts have served as guideposts for putting the Theory of Reality (TOR) together.

One concept that presented itself early on was that it would not be possible to arrive at meaningful answers to questions about the deeper nature of ourselves, the deeper nature of our universe or the deeper nature of reality, by approaching the issues through the lens of a single field. Rather, such answers would require an approach involving an AMALGAMATION of numerous fields and approaches. Within science, the fields of neuroscience and physics take on particular importance, yet these are augmented and amplified by other sciences, and science itself is complemented and informed by what have largely been thought of as metaphysical and spiritual issues and approaches.

The amalgamation of fields and approaches has often been exceedingly difficult in human endeavor. Individuals have generally tended to approach life and its various issues and questions from a certain vantage point which often relates to a particular field of one's training. This, in turn, has often led to a lack of open-mindedness and to defending one approach AGAINST another rather than to finding the common denominators that define how the different approaches COMPLEMENT one another. So instead of framing the issue as "science vs. spirituality" or "neuroscience vs. physics," for example, and detailing how each field might compete with or detract from another, we need to look carefully at how each of these areas INFORMS the others. Without recognizing the nature and scope of these intersections, we miss a big part of the whole.

Another important concept that presented itself was that offering others tools and techniques to empower themselves and to find their own answers was an even more profound way to be of help than merely putting forward a set of answers. Such tools and techniques can help facilitate a deep level of higher understanding and can serve as corridors to enhanced creativity, effectiveness and fulfillment in life.

Although this book represents an ardent attempt at concisely distilling, combining and presenting key elements to allow readers to "put it all together" and achieve a higher understanding of ourselves and our universe, by its nature, no amount of description in human language will ever be complete, and it will be important and useful for each reader to not only actively come to his or her own understanding of these issues but also build upon this understanding with tools and techniques such as those described in this book.

One further concept that emanates beautifully from the field of medicine involves the importance of emphasizing the potential therapeutic and practical value of putting together new scientific concepts and ideas. It became an important focus of this book not merely to present a theory for scientists and others to comprehend abstractly, but rather to combine scientific theoretical concepts with practical applications of this knowledge to be of help in one's day-to-day life. The entire second half of this book is devoted to providing a number of tools and techniques for this purpose.

Ultimately, in order for us to evolve and become more fully aware of the expanded reality within which we exist, we will need to invoke something within us which reaches beyond materialism. We will need to recognize and use our higher capabilities to expand upon a purely materialistic approach. Such an eventuality need not take anything away from the materialistic aspects of science and medicine that have already been delineated, but rather, should add to and build upon what has been delineated.

It is no coincidence that such a large number of the most influential pioneers in physics who helped catalyze the last major paradigm shift in the early twentieth century from classical physics to relativity and quantum physics (including Planck, Jeans, Einstein, Eddington, Schrödinger, De Broglie, Pauli and Heisenberg) ALL evolved beyond a purely materialistic approach in their conceptualizations of reality and wrote about it extensively at various points in their careers and lives. We, as a scientific community, as a society, and as a species, would be wise to follow their example.

EDITORIAL NOTE

The reader will note that the presentation of the Theory of Reality in this book contains several instances of repetition and/or overlap of content from one area to another.

This style was incorporated by design so that each section could be more self-contained, allowing readers to start and end wherever they may wish in a particular reading session.

Such a style also carries with it the potential benefit of having the reader experience certain content in a variety of different contexts which can allow enhanced understanding of specific subject matter.

THEORY *of* REALITY OVERVIEW

The Theory of Reality (TOR) combines key elements of neuroscience, physics and metaphysical science to deepen our understanding of ourselves and our universe with the goal of helping anyone to live a happier, more successful and more fulfilling life. In 2005, the journal *Science* published a special anniversary issue delineating 125 questions that scientists have so far failed to answer. The most important unanswered question was "What is the universe made of?" and the second most important was "What is the biological basis of consciousness?" The Theory of Reality provides answers to these questions.

The TOR is organized into three major components: You, Your Journey and The Territory. It starts by describing and defining the core identity of each individual beyond the body and brain since the fundamental nature of individual consciousness is the same as the fundamental nature of the universe and All That Is.

Coming to recognize the body and brain as temporary vehicles rather than one's core identity is fundamental to any form of spiritual enlightenment. Looking inward (with or without the assistance of numerous existing tools) rather than looking outward for meaning and answers is also paramount. An active vs. passive process—and charting and navigating one's own journey give rise to "knowing" or "experiencing" vs. "believing" these fundamentals, and allow higher understanding, uncommon creativity, and greater effectiveness, happiness and fulfillment to unfold.

The universe is a unified living process rather than a collection of separate objects. Consciousness is *not* contained within matter or the world—it *contains* all matter and the world. Intelligent, informative consciousness is fundamental to all matter, and, although things can still be part of an individual whole while possessing their own unique qualities, our tendency to fragment the world and see ourselves as separate from the universe, from the earth, and from other human and nonhuman beings is responsible for many problems in science and society and ultimately is responsible for our neither being at peace as a species nor as a society. The TOR provides the underpinnings for a different perspective and an approach for personal and societal transformation.

THEORY *of* REALITY CONDENSED MESSAGES

1. Your brain does not create your consciousness or your thoughts.
2. You are not your brain or body—they are temporary vehicles rather than your core identity.
3. The brain is both wondrous and highly limiting.
4. You can exist and function without your brain.
5. The you beyond your brain is indestructible, even by death.
6. Your subconscious mind is far more conscious and far more capable than what is normally thought of as your conscious mind.
7. It is important to get to know your deeper identity (higher self).
8. Brain activity in itself cannot explain or account for consciousness.
9. The brain *facilitates* consciousness and our expression and application of consciousness to this plane of existence, but it does not *create* consciousness.

10. During life on this plane, humans and nonhumans perceive with the physical senses while the brain functions as an interface to nonphysical levels.

11. NDEs (Near-Death Experiences) are valid, real phenomena and not hallucinations, seizures or some other aberration.

12. NDEs (including experiencing, thinking about, seeing, remembering and reporting details and events near and far away) occur with no demonstrable brain function and flat EEGs.

13. Blind people can see during NDEs and OOBEs (Out-of-Body Experiences) with no functioning brain visual system.

14. Understanding the genesis and significance of NDEs and other related phenomena facilitates access to important new corridors of scientific and spiritual understanding.

15. Peak Experiences (PEs) generally involve seconds to minutes in which one feels the highest levels of peace, connectedness, happiness, harmony and possibility.

16. Numerous techniques that can facilitate Peak Experiences or otherwise deeply enhance one's creative, intellectual, visionary or integrative understanding and/or capabilities can serve as useful tools for one's spiritual adventures and journeys.

17. A "spiritual adventure" can generally be visualized with a circular/cyclical display consisting of several components, each leading to and/or fueling the next, including *Understanding, Centering, Equipping, Charting, Navigating, Discovering, Sharing,* and *Assisting Others*—which in turn leads to further *Understanding* and to a new cycle.

18. We are all empowered to embark upon the wildest, most fascinating and most fulfilling spiritual adventures that we can imagine.

19. Looking inward (with or without the assistance of numerous available tools) rather than outward for the answers to one's most profound questions is critical.

20. Anyone can access and be guided by one's higher self.

21. Actively charting and navigating one's own journey and adventures gives rise to "knowing" or "experiencing" vs. passively "believing" spiritual fundamentals—allowing higher understanding, uncommon creativity, and greater effectiveness, happiness and fulfillment to unfold.

22. Increasing one's coherence by one or more of numerous methods—ranging from esoteric metaphysical techniques to relatively simple ways to enhance one's resilience and equanimity—can greatly enhance one's neurological, psychological and spiritual capabilities.

23. The universe is a deeply unified living process rather than a collection of separate objects.

24. Consciousness is *not* contained within matter or the world—it *contains* all matter and the world.

25. Intelligent, informative consciousness is fundamental to all matter and all that exists.

26. Our tendency to fragment our world and to see ourselves as separate from the universe, the earth and from other human and nonhuman beings is at the root of our neither being at peace as a species nor as a society.

27. The TOR provides the underpinnings to address the most basic universal questions of humankind—Who are we? Where are we going? How do we fit into the universe?—and an approach for personal and societal transformation.

THEORY *of* REALITY
FUNDAMENTAL DESCRIPTION

The Theory of Reality (TOR) combines key elements of neuroscience, physics and metaphysical science to deepen our understanding of ourselves and our universe with the goal of helping anyone to live a happier, more successful and more fulfilling life. In 2005, the journal *Science* published a special anniversary issue delineating 125 questions that scientists have so far failed to answer. The most important unanswered question was "What is the universe made of?" and the second most important was "What is the biological basis of consciousness?" The Theory of Reality provides answers to these questions.

YOU

The brain is both wondrous and highly limiting—it does not create your thoughts or your consciousness but rather *facilitates* your thoughts and consciousness and their application and expression to this plane of existence. It acts as both a receiver and a transducer of a variety of consciousness-based information. During life on this plane, most humans (and nonhumans) perceive with the senses while the brain functions as an interface between our "outer" or particle-based materialistic world and our "inner" deeper subconscious or wave-based non-materialistic reality. One's subconscious mind is far more conscious and far more capable than what one normally thinks of as one's conscious mind.

We are intelligent energy forms inhabiting our brains and bodies and, like electrons and everything else on this physical plane, we have two very different aspects to our reality: (1) physical bodies and (2) a blur of interference patterns enfolded throughout the cosmos. You are not your body and brain. Getting to know your deeper conscious self and coming to recognize that your body and brain (and all the elements that you "identify" with on this plane such as your name and occupation) are mere vehicles and tools for temporarily expressing the real (and indestructible) you—and *knowing* (as opposed to passively believing) the above—are fundamental to what has been referred to as spiritual enlightenment.

Conventional neurological science has clearly shown that brain function *correlates* with states of consciousness, which are in turn *correlated* with various brain structures. However, these observations in no way prove that the brain or any brain structure *creates* consciousness. The innermost essence of ourselves is pure consciousness which is the innermost essence of all that exists and, in this sense, (particularly in view of the holographic type of organization underlying the universe) we are all indeed one with All That Is (defined by many as God or the Divine).

Consciousness is the canvas upon which mind generates our impressions—it is not PART of the impressions. Therefore we do not "see" consciousness "out there" with the other apparently material "things." The vast majority of the individuals involved in consciousness research, including neurologists and other neuroscientists, psychiatrists, psychologists and philosophers, are still of the opinion that consciousness arises entirely from the matter that constitutes one's brain. This is a materialistic or reductionist viewpoint. Such a circumstance would mean that all of our behavior would be the inevitable outcome of nerve cell activity in the brain and that free will would not truly exist. According to this viewpoint, our consciousness would essentially behave like a materialistic machine controlled by classical physics and chemistry. There is not only substantial evidence for our ability to exist and function very well without the brain, but there is also enough compelling evidence to prove that brain activity in itself cannot explain or account for consciousness. Consciousness is *not* contained within matter or the world—it *contains* all matter and the world.

YOUR JOURNEY

From the time humans are born on this planet, they are taught to look outward and to look to various institutions—academic institutions, economic institutions, political institutions, social institutions, etc. for meaning and for answers. In reality, they need to look inward for answers. Everything that is needed, including God (All That Is), is inward. Your journey in this arena leads to a new understanding—a new beginning. It is an active process, and it is important for you to chart your own way. It is a journey to higher understanding, greater creativity/intelligence and greater effectiveness. You are empowered to explore, find and do all of this without dependence upon or indebtedness to others (or fear of taking your own unique path) through knowing the "inner" you, the more authentic you—your most reliable and capable guide.

Near-Death Experiences (NDEs) are valid, real phenomena and not hallucinations, seizures or some other aberration. NDEs (including experiencing, thinking about, seeing, remembering and reporting details and events near and far away) occur with no demonstrable brain function and flat electroencephalograms (EEGs). Blind people can see during NDEs and other types of Out-of-Body Experiences (OOBEs) with no functioning brain visual system. One of the greatest values of these experiences is that one subsequently KNOWS as opposed to BELIEVES that he or she can and ultimately *will* exist (and that one can think, see, remember and otherwise function) independently from the physical body and brain, which is fundamental to higher-level spiritual thought.

NDEs, OOBEs and other related phenomena and techniques—Connecting with One's Higher Self (CWOHS), After Death Contact (ADC), Past Life Recall/Regression (PLR), various types of yoga and meditation, lucid dreams/dream control, visualization, hypnosis, contemplation/prayer, etc.—generally involve focused states of consciousness and can be important tools for enabling all kinds of understanding—scientific, spiritual, overall creativity, music, art, relationships, etc. Any of these phenomena and techniques can be associated with Peak Experiences (PEs) which generally involve seconds to minutes in which one feels the highest levels of peace, connectedness, happiness, harmony and possibility. They often are pivotal moments in a person's life and are often associated with key insights, "waves of understanding," and/or instantaneous packages of ideas ("thought balls"). These are valuable and useful phenomena which should be encouraged and instigated if one is so inclined.

Einstein observed, "The intellect has little to do on the road to discovery. There comes a leap in consciousness, call it intuition or what you will, and the solution comes to you and you don't know how or why." Going from random incoherent thought to coherent (focused) consciousness can be as powerful as going from incandescent (incoherent) light to a laser beam, particularly given the holographic organization of the universe (a visual hologram can be created with a laser but not with incandescent light). By achieving a highly focused level of awareness, anyone can tap into normally unconscious or latent abilities. Moreover, achieving specialized states of consciousness may allow the individual to access hierarchical levels of information *enfolded* within the basic structure of the universe.

It is also important to note that increasing one's coherence does not necessarily require accomplishing any particular "difficult" feat or austere lifestyle—or a specifically prescribed altered state of consciousness or OOBE. In general, factors that increase one's *resilience* and *equanimity* also tend to increase one's coherence. Resilience is the capacity following adverse or stressful events to adapt to (and even thrive in) the resulting challenges and changing circumstances. Such a capacity proactively insulates and protects individuals from a variety of anxiety disorders and depression. Similarly, equanimity is the inner strength and stability to experience well-being and confidence in the *eye of the storm*—enabling one to maintain a relaxed body and calm, balanced mind regardless of the circumstances. It allows one to remain centered and to see the big picture with perspective and patience. Factors that are generally enjoyable for individuals that also increase one's resilience and equanimity include laughter, music, intimacy (including friendship and sexual intimacy), spiritual exploration and understanding, and sleep. Enhancing these factors can be a fun and compelling way to increase one's coherence while optimizing brain and neurological function as well as psychological health.

THE TERRITORY

Intelligent, informative consciousness is fundamental to all matter. God (All That Is) is within all of us and within every Consciousness Unit that makes up everything in the universe. All are one. Everything in the universe is part of a continuum, and it is meaningless to talk of the universe as comprised of parts. Although things can still be part of an individual whole while possessing their own unique qualities, our tendency to fragment our world and see ourselves as separate from the universe, from the earth, from other human and nonhuman beings is responsible for many problems in science and society and ultimately is at the root of our neither being at peace as a species nor as a society.

The deepest reality is the reality of pure consciousness—it underlies progressively coarser (more materialistic) levels of reality that are enfolded into the same time and space. Pure consciousness is a more subtle form than matter (and energy, of course) which is present in various degrees of unfoldment in all matter. Consciousness is the fundamental "wave aspect" in deeper dimensions which manifests as the various dimensions and attributes of the physical world including space, time, matter, energy, sensory forms, locality and causality which can all be thought of as "particle aspects."

The most fundamental aspect or "fabric" of the universe is a consciousness/information/intelligence field (which we will refer to as the "C Field" for simplicity) that is made up of individual consciousness/information/intelligence units (C Units) present everywhere in the universe independent of human intent and action. Access to the more universal information/intelligence aspects of the C Field (which is enhanced by increased coherence and guided by an individual's resonance—i.e., like attracts like on a thought/consciousness level) enhances creativity, medical and scientific discovery, and understanding of anything and everything including profound and not so profound spiritual matters.

The C Field links things (subatomic particles, atoms, molecules, organisms, planets, solar systems, as well as the mind and consciousness associated with these things) regardless of how far they are from one another and regardless of how much "time" has passed since connections were created between them. The C Field not only *connects* all that exists, but it also *informs* (with stored and shared intelligent information) and thereby *"guides"* all that exists; it acts as a *mirror* for the thoughts, emotions and beliefs within us; and it is nonlocal and holographic in nature. Moreover, multiple dimensions are enfolded into the same time and space which are all connected by this same fundamental field. The materialistic dimension that we see here is the most coarse and crude of the dimensions. Deeper dimensions become increasingly responsive to thought.

The universe is a unified living process rather than a collection of separate objects. Individual consciousness is the same as the essential nature of the entire cosmos. The building blocks of the universe are Consciousness Units, or C Units, infused with information, intelligence, purpose and guidance at every level. These can also be partially characterized as units of perception or experience. In the quantum physics subatomic (smaller than atoms) world of virtual particles, "things" don't exist in material form but rather as fleeting displays of tendencies and superimposed possibilities with nonlocality and indeterminacy. This is the nature of pure consciousness. The universe is interactive at all levels of existence, from the smallest C Unit to the largest galaxy.

Intelligence (broad sense) is the ability of any system to make connections that are meaningful and helpful to that system in its relations with other systems. Any self-organizing system must be imbued with some level of intelligence. Simpler systems such as individual cells (which are still enormously complex) make up larger and even more complex systems (organs, circulatory systems); which constitute larger systems (oaks, ducks, tuna, sheep, humans); which make up groves, flocks, herds, villages; which make up forests, rivers, ecosystems; which make up planets; which make up galaxies. The intelligence of this universal wholeness embraces all apparent parts down to the tiniest, and lives within all parts as their intelligence. The universal intelligence can only be sensed non-dualistically (best accomplished outside the brain) through intuitive receptivity—it is beyond our usual human experience and capability.

Science meeting spirituality is key. The science behind NDEs, OOBEs and other related phenomena allows a quantum leap in human understanding of ourselves and our universe. Science and spirituality can *combine* (rather than conflict) to open new vistas, provide self-actualization, and optimize neurologic performance. Neuroscience meeting physics to expand and enhance each other is also key. Both neuroscience and physics need to evolve into the 21ST century and beyond. They are both slowed by the inertia of outdated and limited concepts and paradigms. Until these disciplines incorporate what are now thought of as largely spiritual and metaphysical dimensions, our models will only be able to account for the most materialistic and mundane aspects of our lives and will miss many of the most important aspects of existence.

THEORY *of* REALITY CONSCIOUSNESS PARADIGM

1. The word "consciousness" is used in many different ways which should be distinguished for clarity. (A) Within conventional neurology and the neurosciences, physicians and scientists generally refer to *states* of consciousness which characterize how awake and responsive one is to this material world. There are waking or responsive states of consciousness, as well as a variety of less responsive and unresponsive states of consciousness (including sleep states, coma and numerous coma-like states) that have been described and defined. These various states of consciousness correlate with and are dependent upon how well the brain is functioning. (B) Consciousness can also refer to the *contents* of one's *brain's memories* which, in this context, comprise the laid-down memories and experiences that one's brain can extract from the part of the C Field with which it resonates. Access to these contents can vary greatly at different points in life and with a variety of neurological and other medical conditions which generally impair access.

(C) Consciousness can also refer to the *faculty* of being able to experience an inner world—and thinking, perceiving, seeing and remembering—which can occur *when the brain is not functioning* (e.g., NDEs). This form of consciousness does not correlate with nor depend upon brain function. (D) Consciousness can additionally be used to refer to the *contents of one's deeper self's memories and experiences* which are all stored in their entirety without errors in the C Field and which are always available without retrieval errors to one's deeper self. Access to these contents is neither dependent upon the brain nor is it impaired by brain pathology. These contents are accessed and reviewed completely and instantaneously in the life review process during NDEs. (E) When the term "consciousness" is used in the context of C Unit (Consciousness Unit) or C Field (Consciousness Field), it refers to the basic (fundamental) building block and fabric of all that exists in both the deeper and physical realms (the physical is derived from the deeper realms as described above). Conventional neuroscience recognizes and can account for A and B above, which are fundamentally materialistic, but generally does not recognize and cannot account for C, D and E.

2. One of the core components of the TOR is that it identifies consciousness not as something that merely emanates from the human brain but rather as the fundamental fabric of ourselves and our universe.

3. What we refer to as "matter" is the aspect that we perceive when we look at a person, nonhuman animal, plant or an atom from the *outside*—"consciousness" is the aspect we obtain when we look at the same thing from the *inside*.

4. The commonly held viewpoint that consciousness arises entirely from the matter that constitutes the brain reflects a materialistic perspective. It would mean that all of our thoughts and

behavior would be the inevitable outcome of nerve cell activity in the brain and that free will would not truly exist.

5. As described above, consciousness constitutes a form of canvas upon which mind generates our impressions. It is not part of the impressions themselves. Consequently, we do not see consciousness "out there" with the other apparently material "things." These factors have been at the root of a long history of enigmatic confusion relative to the so-called "hard question" in physics and philosophy—namely "How does consciousness arise from matter?" It cannot and does not. Consciousness is not contained within matter or the world—it *contains* all matter and the world.

6. Pure consciousness (as referenced in application E above) is a more subtle form than matter and energy. It is the fundamental "wave aspect" in deeper dimensions, which manifests as the various dimensions and attributes of the physical world including space, time, matter, energy, sensory forms, locality and causality, which can all be thought of as "particle aspects." Consicousness is present in various degrees of unfoldment in all matter. It can be completely unmanifested (undifferentiated), fully manifested or anywhere in between in the formative process depending upon the dimension (plane of existence) and the state of creative manifestation. Those "particle aspects" referenced above, which we can fully observe, constitute examples of manifested consciousness on this physical plane of existence.

7. In terms of general human perception, space, time, matter and energy seem to be fundamental aspects of the physical world, but they are in reality fundamental aspects of the impressions (forms) which are appearing in consciousness.

8. The brain not only transcribes information from the deeper level of pure consciousness to construct a time-space duality-oriented physical world, *but also limits and puts a ceiling on* our

perception of pure consciousness, All That Is (defined by many as God or the Divine), and higher (deeper/less dense) planes of existence that are enfolded into the same time/space.

9. As individual humans living on this plane and in this dimension, we experience ourselves to be located around a central point within our head. This is part of our "perception" that the brain, as a transcriber, helps create for us in our "image of reality" in this dimension. In reality our consciousness is not located anywhere in the world.

10. The brain transcribes wave forms from "deeper" reality via wave function collapse, which allows us to experience, translate and communicate our impressions on this plane in this dimension. Such transcription is not needed in other dimensions.

11. The physical or "particle" aspect of our consciousness, which we experience as waking consciousness on this plane, is created by collapsing wave functions in nonlocal space. It is this particle aspect that is observable and measurable by various neurological studies such as EEG and fMRI. Memory is stored as wave functions in "nonlocal space" in connection with a consciousness field (C Field) so that there is essentially infinite storage capacity, and so that the memories are never lost but are accessible everywhere independent of time and space. Memories are available to the brain via its *resonance* with nonlocal consciousness or the C Field. Regarding the information transfer via resonance, overall brain function can be likened to a quantum hologram and the brain to a quantum processing unit operating in parallel, capable of decoding information that enters nonlocally.

12. The building blocks of the world and the universe are not atomic structures such as atoms, protons, neutrons and electrons but rather Consciousness Units (C Units). The essential units and features of consciousness are built into the universe

at the most basic level—and they repeat in scale holographically. Consciousness is the fabric of the universe, a quantum superposition of possibilities, the essence of which constitutes a fine structural field (C Field) that pervades everything that exists.

13. The Principle of Unity starts from the ONE Consciousness and describes everything as derived from the ONE via a process involving visualization, imagination and knowingness not unlike our own human latent creative abilities. In the holographic organizational scaling process, one continues to find the ONE throughout the rest of creation moving forward. Part of the reason we are here is to learn this process of creation and to participate as co-creators.

14. If indeed the essence of consciousness can be found in everything, everywhere, then our own essence and the essence of EVERYTHING is divine—something which upon reflection can awaken one's deep sense of wonder about the universe.

15. It is meaningless to talk of the universe as comprised of parts. Everything in the universe is part of a continuum. Intelligent, informative consciousness is part of all matter. All That Is (God or the Divine) is within all of us and within every Consciousness Unit that makes up everything in the universe. The universe is a unified living process rather than a collection of separate objects.

16. The deepest reality is the reality of pure consciousness—it underlies progressively coarser (more materialistic) levels of reality which are enfolded into the same time and space.

17. A consciousness/information/intelligence field (C Field) comprised of individual consciousness/information/intelligence units (C Units) constitutes the most fundamental aspect or "fabric" of the universe. It is present everywhere in the universe independent of human intent and action. Access to the more

universal aspects of the C Field can generally enhance one's creativity and higher understanding, and can be associated with various forms of insight and discovery.

18. The C Field links things (subatomic particles, atoms, molecules, organisms, planets, solar systems, as well as the mind and consciousness associated with these things) regardless of how far they are from one another and regardless of how much "time" has passed since connections were created between them. The C Field not only *connects* all that exists, but it also *informs* (with stored and shared intelligent information) and thereby "*guides*" all that exists; it acts as a *mirror* for the thoughts, emotions and beliefs within us; and it is nonlocal and holographic in nature. Moreover, multiple dimensions are enfolded into the same time and space which are all connected by this same fundamental field. The materialistic dimension that we see here is the most coarse and crude of the dimensions.

19. The fundamental nature of individual consciousness is the same as the essential nature of the entire cosmos. The universe is interactive at all levels of existence, from the smallest C Unit to the largest galaxy. The building blocks of the universe are Consciousness Units, or C Units, infused with information, intelligence, purpose and guidance at every level. These can also be partially characterized as units of perception or experience. In the quantum physics subatomic world of virtual particles, "things" don't exist in material form but rather as fleeting displays of tendencies and superimposed possibilities with nonlocality and indeterminacy. This is the nature of pure consciousness.

ABOUT *the* TOR KEY EVIDENCE CATEGORIES

There are 11 key categories of evidence that underlie the TOR. Three of these are primary (more fundamental) and eight are secondary (relatively less fundamental but still of key significance).

All of these categories overlap, interrelate and interface with each other considerably, and the reader will note extensive cross-referencing in the text to emphasize areas where these aspects occur. Understanding the information and concepts within the 11 categories and how they relate to one another allows one to establish a deeper vision of the whole and to more profoundly address three of the most fundamental questions that we all have as part of humankind—Who am I? Where am I going? and How do I fit into the universe? These questions correspond to the three organizational components of the TOR (You, Your Journey and The Territory) referenced above in the Overview and Fundamental Description sections.

In other words, the 11 evidence categories are designed to try to help one to "put it all together" and, in the process, to better understand the nature of consciousness and the nature of the universe which are interwoven. Individual consciousness is of the same essence as the fabric of the entire cosmos.

As stated previously, by its nature, no amount of description of this sort will ever be complete, and it will be important and useful for each individual to not only actively come to their own understanding of the areas discussed in the evidence categories but also proceed to reflect and build upon this understanding with various verbal and nonverbal tools and techniques such as those described in the Tools and Techniques section of this book.

The order of the primary and secondary evidence categories does not necessarily imply any graded importance, but rather is designed to help the reader build on earlier categories as later categories are presented.

For those readers who are less inclined toward science and scientific explanations, it is entirely acceptable to skip any or all of the evidence categories contained within this section and move directly into the more practical day-to-day applications of this scientific knowledge base which are contained within the Anatomy of a Spiritual Adventure and Tools and Techniques sections that follow.

KEY EVIDENCE CATEGORIES

TOR—PRIMARY CATEGORIES OF EVIDENCE

1. Evidence that Near-Death Experiences are valid, real phenomena and not hallucinations, seizures or some other aberration.
2. Evidence for our ability to exist and function separately without the brain
3. Evidence that brain activity in and of itself cannot account for consciousness.

TOR—SECONDARY CATEGORIES OF EVIDENCE

1. Evidence for intelligence outside the human brain—down to the electron, photon and C Unit levels.

2. Evidence for coherence and resonance as underlying mechanisms for communication at multiple levels.

3. Evidence for a holographic type of organization underlying our brains and our universe.

4. Evidence for a C Field as a basic underlying matrix or fabric for reality (as we experience it here and in other dimensions) and for some unit of this (C Unit) as the most fundamental building block of the universe.

5. Evidence for various types of Peak Experiences and other related phenomena being associated with discoveries, creativity, and other types of uncommon insight and understanding.

6. Evidence for other "finer" levels of existence enfolded into the same space and time as this physical plane.

7. Evidence for particle and wave aspects of subatomic structures (as documented by physicists) and for how these components parallel the particle and wave aspects of consciousness, energy and matter.

8. Evidence that "empty space" is not at all empty and that it instead contains an incredibly vast amount of energy and provides insight into what is hidden from our materialistic senses and a materialistic conceptualization of the universe.

A. THEORY *of* REALITY PRIMARY EVIDENCE

1. Evidence that Near-Death Experiences (NDEs) Are Valid, Real Phenomena and Not Hallucinations, Seizures or Some Other Aberration

Many mainstream scientists have expended considerable effort and energy trying to relegate NDEs to the arena of invalid illusions, hoaxes or other aberrations. In the process, an extensive list of alternative explanations has been advanced to cast doubt upon the significance of these phenomena. Such alternative explanations are largely rooted in a purely materialistic approach to science and fall into two major categories—namely psychological and neurophysiological explanations. It is important to review the evidence underlying each of these alternative explanations and to assess the likelihood that any or all of them may be relevant.

Note: Readers who are unfamiliar with the characteristic features and potential benefits of NDEs are encouraged to review the section on NDEs under Tools and Techniques for a description of these aspects prior to reviewing the evidence that follows here.

PSYCHOLOGICAL EXPLANATIONS

1. Hallucinations

Over the years, many have suggested that NDEs are simply hallucinations. In clinical practice, hallucinations are defined as sensory phenomena that an individual perceives as real that are not rooted in reality. The fact that individuals having NDEs have Out-of-Body Experiences (OOBEs) which include verifiable accurate perceptions based in this reality means that an NDE is, by definition, not a hallucination. Hallucinations require a functioning brain and clinically involve a great deal of brain activity, whereas NDEs are well documented to occur in the context of no brain activity. Clinically, hallucinations are more commonly associated with psychiatric disorders such as schizophrenia, or with excessive use of (or withdrawal from) alcohol and other drugs. Conversely, people with NDEs are generally emotionally stable and have not used drugs, alcohol or other mind-altering medications before their experience. Hallucinations tend to be very unique and personal phenomena, whether visual, auditory, olfactory (smell) or taste. In contrast to NDEs they do not contain universal elements. Moreover, hallucinations are clearly not associated with the types of lasting spiritual advancement and enhancements in various intuitive capabilities that are common among those experiencing NDEs.

2. Depersonalization

Depersonalization refers to a psychological state in which individuals are detached from their own identity and surroundings with feelings of alienation, unreality, fear, panic, emptiness and other unpleasant emotions. In contrast, individuals having an NDE experience feelings of peace and love, have an enhanced perception of reality, are completely aware of their identity and have very clear and lucid thoughts and memories. In addition, NDEs and OOBEs have not been clinically reported in cases of clinical depersonalization.

3. Dissociation

Dissociation refers to a psychological defense mechanism whereby one's emotions are separated and detached from traumatic events in order to postpone or escape having to deal with the frightening reality of the trauma. It involves, by definition, "the disruption of the usually integrated functions of identity, memory, and consciousness." In contrast, individuals experiencing NDEs have no evidence to suggest feeling traumatized or wanting to avoid or escape a trauma. They have lucid thinking, great awareness and memory function, and a completely intact sense of identity.

4. Expectations, Wishful Thinking, Fear of Death

Many have suggested that NDEs are phenomena that individuals create based upon their cultural and religious expectations to shield them from the fear of impending death. However, individuals who have never heard or read about NDEs have the same types of experiences as those who are familiar with NDEs. For many, their NDE does not match their prior expectations of death whatsoever. Moreover, their experiences tend to be virtually identical whether or not they believe in life after death and regardless of religious affiliation or degree of participation in religious ceremonies. (Although NDE research has revealed some relatively minor differences in the frequency and content of some NDE elements based upon culture, geography and religious affiliation, the meaning and impact are essentially unchanged.) Finally, individuals who did not expect to die (such as those undergoing a surgical procedure fully expecting to survive) report the same types of NDEs as those expecting to die.

5. Fantasy, Imaginative Reconstructions, Lucky Guesses, Prior Knowledge/Memories of Circumstances, Semiconscious Perception

There is no evidence to suggest that NDErs were more likely to have fantasy-prone personalities than non-NDErs prior to their experiences. Children tend to fantasize more than adults in the general population, yet the NDEs reported by children have been essentially identical to those of adults. Reports of occurrences during NDEs by individuals with no demonstrable brain function have included numerous verifiable facts that they could not have possibly seen or heard with their normal senses, either in the same room or at a great distance. Blind people (including those who have been blind from birth and who do not have any visual images associated with their dreams) can see and read during NDEs (and other types of OOBEs) with no brain function and obvious preexisting nonfunctioning brain visual systems. When cardiac arrest patients who did not experience NDEs have been asked to describe their resuscitation, they almost invariably (20 of 25 patients) make at least one major error in the description. In contrast, not one of the 32 cardiac arrest patients who did experience an NDE during their resuscitation made major errors in reporting the details of their procedures (Sabom 1982). It is also highly unlikely that any of these alternative explanations would be associated with the profound and moving experiences and emotions that patients relate even years after the event and with the profound spiritual benefits that follow the event which most NDErs experience.

6. Personality Traits/Disorders

Available data suggest no antecedent personality disorders or specific common personality traits that would explain a person's likelihood for having an NDE. NDEs generally occur in psychologically stable individuals who are able to function well in their lives and who are not different from those in a population control group who have not had an NDE except for age. (NDEs do tend to occur more frequently in younger individuals, which is not surprising given that older individuals are more likely to remain "dead.")

7. Dreams

Although certain features of dreams are in some ways analogous to NDEs, individuals with NDEs are very clear in their description of the NDE as fundamentally different from any dream they ever had. Unlike NDEs, dreams do not have the type of fixed elements that are present across all ages, regardless of a person's gender, marital status, social class, nationality, religion, spiritual beliefs, and social class. Dreams are generally very personal and highly dependent upon the individual and their life circumstances. Dreams are generally easily forgotten whereas NDEs are not. People who have been blind since birth who do not have any visual images associated with dreams can see and form visual memories during NDEs. Dreams are generally not associated with the types of spiritual advancement and enhanced intuitive capabilities that commonly occur (and remain indefinitely) after NDEs.

8. Memories of Birth

Some have suggested that the experience of moving through a tunnel toward light and experiencing a "heroic figure" bathed in light could simply mean that NDEs are memories of a human's birth. However, research comparing tunnel and OOBE experiences among those delivered vaginally and those delivered via cesarean section revealed no significant difference between the two groups (Blackmore 1983). Moreover, such an explanation for NDEs could not account for numerous other aspects of NDEs, including life reviews, visions of deceased relatives and friends, or other wonderful peaceful visions of unearthly environments. Also, it is extremely rare for an individual to be able to remember birth, and in cases where any recollection exists, it is limited, blurred and fragmented at best in contrast to the types of lucid details related following NDEs.

9. Deceit

Some have suggested that NDErs are simply lying about their experiences in an effort to present themselves as interesting or impressive to others. Yet NDErs often will keep quiet for years about their experiences out of fear that they may be seen as mentally imbalanced or hallucinatory. When they do relate their experiences, it is often after some reassurance of understanding or interest on the part of the listener. When one visits directly with individuals who have had an NDE, it becomes almost immediately apparent that they are reflecting genuine emotions and that they are having to struggle to find the right words to explain their experiences in usual human terms. Again, individuals who have no prior written or spoken knowledge about NDEs relate virtually the same types of experiences with numerous common elements (which are independent of multiple demographic characteristics) as those familiar with NDE accounts. This explanation for NDEs would almost certainly NOT be associated with the types of spiritual advancement and enhanced intuitive capabilities that have been documented following NDEs.

10. Psychological Effects of Medications

Some have suggested that certain kinds of medications administered to dying patients such as morphine or other strong pain killers might cause NDEs by causing an individual to become delusional. However, NDEs are commonly reported by individuals who use no medication whatsoever and/or have not been on medication at the time of death. Such an explanation would also not be compatible with an enhanced perception of reality, accelerated thinking, enhanced memory and complete awareness of one's identity. NDE studies that have utilized medication effect as a variable to account for

NDEs have found no evidence that medication is responsible for causing NDEs.

11. Breakdown of Body Image and Model of Reality

Some have suggested that NDErs are using whatever information is available to build a new body image so that they can get back to normal. They have also suggested that these types of memory images are generally from a bird's-eye view, suggesting that this could account for the individual mistakenly thinking that they are outside their body. Yet to reconstruct a new body image and perceive it in our physical body would require a functioning brain, and NDEs are well documented to occur with no identifiable brain function whatsoever. What little research that exists regarding "observer" (bird's-eye) vs. "field" (from the perspective of the experiencer) memory in no way confirms that the bird's-eye view aspect relates to building a new reality from memories. Again, NDEs are associated with enhanced perceptions of reality, complete awareness of one's identity, intact and enhanced memory, and access to more universal wisdom, all of which would not be expected from this alternative explanation. NDEs are also associated with verifiable facts based in the reality of this physical dimension that individuals could not have possibly seen or heard with their usual senses (see #5 above), including details at great distances that occurred at the time of no identifiable brain function and visual details reported by congenitally blind individuals.

NEUROPHYSIOLOGICAL EXPLANATIONS

1. Hypoxia/Anoxia (Oxygen Deficiency)

Many have suggested that a severe and life-threatening lack of oxygen to the brain causes impaired brain activity (which precedes loss of all brain activity) and that NDEs are the result of a sputtering or shutting down sequence which includes the release of endorphins (see below #4) that cause hallucinations (see above #1 under Psychological Explanations) and a sense of peace and tranquility. Yet this circumstance is incompatible with the enhanced, lucid awareness and memories that accompany NDEs. As discussed above, there are numerous reasons why hallucinations are not responsible for NDEs. NDEs and OOBEs can also occur under circumstances such as an imminent traffic accident or in cases of severe depression, neither of which involves a deficiency of oxygen to the brain. The tunnel experience has been explained by some as an oxygen deficiency to the brain's visual cortex or to the eyes. However, such an oxygen deficiency would not explain numerous associated phenomena such as the life review, meeting deceased friends and relatives, the accompanying feeling of moving at high speed, or the perception of peaceful environments or soothing music. Hypoxic/anoxic episodes also generally are accompanied by a LACK of ability to recall clearly and by hazy memories and recall. Transforming life experiences are not associated with hypoxic/anoxic episodes.

2. Seizures/Excessive Electrical Stimulation of the Brain

Some have suggested that seizures may be the underlying cause of NDEs, largely on the basis that certain types of seizures (particularly those involving the temporal lobes of the brain) are sometimes associated with hallucinations (see above #1 under Psychological Explanations), feelings of unreality and being detached from the body, feelings of déjà vu, and memory flashbacks which are often disorganized and random in nature. Yet seizures require brain activity, and NDEs have been well documented during EEG monitoring that shows no brain activity and certainly no seizure activity. Moreover, various components of typical NDEs (including the knowledge that one has died and consequently is no longer confined to one's body, communicating with deceased friends and relatives in another dimension, and a detailed, sequential, organized life review) have not been associated with temporal lobe seizures or any other type of seizure. One's perception during a seizure is generally distorted, which differs considerably from the very lucid, enhanced perception reported with NDEs. In addition, the characteristic features of temporal lobe seizures tend to vary greatly from one individual to another whereas NDEs have remarkably uniform characteristic features. Seizures and other forms of electrical stimulation are clearly not associated with lasting spiritual advancement and enhancements in various intuitive capabilities.

3. Hypercarbia (Excessive Carbon Dioxide)

Excessive levels of carbon dioxide in the blood and brain have been associated with certain symptoms that have led some to believe that this may account for NDEs. In the 1950s, carbon dioxide inhalation was tried as a possible neuropsychiatric therapeutic measure, and some of these patients reported memory flashbacks, a sense of being detached from their bodies, feelings of peace and even images of bright light and/or a tunnel type experience. However, these images and experiences were rare, disorganized and very fragmented unlike the experiences with NDEs. The carbon dioxide experiences also included many other types of symptoms such as muscle twitching and seizure like activity, double or triple vision, perceptions of colored geometric patterns and objects such as musical notes floating by—none of which are associated with NDEs. At least one carefully documented instance exists of a patient experiencing an NDE/OOBE during cardiopulmonary resuscitation with an arterial blood gas sample drawn during the experience that documented *increased* blood oxygen (another refutation of the oxygen deficiency explanation discussed above) and *decreased* blood carbon dioxide (Sabom 1982). While arterial blood levels may arguably not reflect exact levels in the brain, the arterial and brain levels are generally strongly correlated. Overall, the brain is more sensitive to a lack of oxygen than it is to excessive carbon dioxide, and hence many of the same difficulties discussed above in the oxygen deficiency section also apply here.

4. Endorphins

Stress of any kind can be associated with the release of endorphins, which are naturally occurring morphine-like substances that act as neurotransmitters in the brain. They have been associated with feelings of peace and tranquility and hence some have suggested that endorphins may mediate NDEs. However, endorphins have not been associated with the numerous other common features of NDEs, including OOBEs, tunnel experience, perception of a brilliant light or being of light, life review, meeting deceased friends or relatives, conscious return to the body, telepathic communication, and lasting spiritual and intuitive enhancements. Clinically, endorphin effects last several hours whereas most of the above elements stop abruptly after the individual regains consciousness.

5. Ketamine

Some have pointed to the effects of ketamine, a drug that has been used as an anesthetic and blocks NMDA (N-Methyl-D-aspartate) receptors in the brain, to suggest that some similar chemical agent in the brain is responsible for NDEs. Ketamine can produce hallucinations (see above #1 under Psychological Explanations) that are generally frightening and bizarre but may be associated with a sense of detachment. The same refutations discussed above relative to hallucinations apply here. In addition, NDEs are generally not frightening experiences; no naturally occurring ketamine-like substance has been identified in the brain; and a host of other NDE features (such as those listed above in the endorphin discussion) cannot be accounted for by experiences with ketamine. Moreover, Kenneth Ring, a psychologist and noted NDE researcher, reported in 2003, "As to my experiences with ketamine, in my day I took the drug a total of 9 times. My trips were extremely variable and while often transcendent, nothing I experienced, either in content or texture, had any particular overlap with the classic NDE."

6. Psychedelic Drugs

As with ketamine above, a variety of other psychoactive drugs, including LSD, psilocybin, mescaline and DMT (all of which have been known to effect the brain transmitter serotonin), have been implicated as producing some features similar to NDEs including a sense of detachment, OOBEs, feelings of unconditional love, unearthly environments and even encounters with a being of light. However, as with ketamine, the nature of the experience depends a great deal on the mindset of the individual and the individual's earthly surroundings at the time of taking the drug. These drug experiences are extremely variable and are often frightening and confusing in contrast to NDEs. They have not been associated with meeting and communicating with deceased friends or relatives, systematic panoramic instantaneous life reviews, conscious and purposeful return to one's body, or generally enhanced depth of spirituality or intuitive capabilities.

7. Disinhibition of Brain Cells

Some have hypothesized that in the dying brain, a generalized lack of normal inhibition of brain cells causes widespread disorganized excitation of brain cells and that this type of phenomena leads to the experiences of NDEs. This alternative explanation suffers from the same difficulties discussed above in the Seizures/Excessive Electrical Stimulation of the Brain section, including the fact that brain activity is required. Since the presumed mechanism of the neural (brain cell) disinhibition is brain hypoxia or anoxia (lack of oxygen), the explanation also suffers from the types of difficulties discussed above in that section. Moreover, there has heretofore been no clinical evidence to associate various NDE type symptoms with the phenomenon of neural disinhibition.

In addition to the evidence presented above, all of the psychological and neurophysiological alternative explanations are drawn into serious question by the phenomenon of shared death experiences whereby others (including individuals or groups of family members, friends, attending physicians, nurses or other medical personnel) have shared the beginning of a death experience along with the dying individual (Moody 2010). When researchers have compared the features of such experiences (sometimes among multiple surviving witnesses) to the features of NDEs, the results have been strikingly similar. No phenomenon in the dying person's brain physiology or psychological makeup could legitimately account for an individual or group of individuals simultaneously sharing and then subsequently recounting the exact same experience.

All in all, the body of evidence supporting the veracity of NDEs is overwhelming (see also Moody 1976, 2010; Sabom 1982; Greyson 1983, 1987, 1998; Ring 1984, 1998, 2008; Morse 1990, 1992; Holdon 2009; Lommel 2010; Carter 2010 and Long 2010). Given that scientists and others have been searching fervently for the better part of four decades to provide explanations to debunk the significance or "reality" of NDEs, and that, upon closer inspection, none of them are credible, it becomes relevant for science and scientists to embrace this expanded reality (rather than try to ignore it) and to consider carefully the vital insights and opportunities that NDEs and related phenomena offer to all of us as we endeavor to evolve beyond a purely materialistic approach to science and toward a broader understanding of life and existence.

A. THEORY *of* REALITY PRIMARY EVIDENCE

2. Evidence for Our Ability to Exist and Function Separately Without the Brain

1. Near-Death Experiences (NDEs) are valid, real phenomena and not hallucinations, seizures or some other aberration (see TOR Primary Evidence #1 for details).

2. NDEs (including experiencing, thinking about, seeing, remembering, and reporting independently verifiable details and events from near and far away) occur with no demonstrable brain function and flat electroencephalograms (EEGs).

3. Blind people (including those who have been blind from birth and who have never been able to see while awake or in dreams, and who consequently do not have functioning material brain/eye visual systems) can see during NDEs and OOBEs (Out-of-Body Experiences), and have reported independently verifiable details requiring vision during NDEs (which, as above, have been documented with no demonstrable brain function) and OOBEs.

4. Typical NDEs involve normal or enhanced mental acuity and function during a time when brain function is increasingly impaired or absent.

5. With *increasingly impaired* or *absent* brain function, individuals having NDEs perceive that they are dying or dead; have accurate out-of-body views of their own bodies and the surrounding environment; participate in telepathic communication with deceased friends, relatives and/or a being of light or other beings; experience a panoramic, detailed, organized, enlightening, instantaneous life review; form detailed accurate memories; are aware that they can exist and witness events on this physical plane (e.g., things going on in the operating room or several blocks or miles away—with many instances of detailed corroboration of events not accessible to one's biological sense organs while one was apparently out of one's body); consciously decide to "come back" to their earthly bodies; and often experience enhanced spiritual and intuitive capabilities which continue indefinitely after the NDE.

6. The perception of and communication with deceased friends or relatives (during NDEs and otherwise) suggest that these deceased individuals continue to exist (in some form) after their brains and bodies have essentially disintegrated (and certainly after brain and body material functions have ceased).

7. Further evidence that deceased individuals continue to exist in some form after their bodies and brains cease to function can be found in studies of Past-Life Recall/Regression (PLR) suggestive of reincarnation. Psychiatrist Ian Stevenson (1974, 1997) at the University of Virginia has carried out extensive systematic research over more than three decades involving over 3,000 children (generally ages 2–6) from 12 countries with spontaneous, vivid memories of past-life experiences. These experiences have included sites, persons and events that these individuals have not and could not have encountered in their present life-

time, with details such as names of their previous spouse and children, specific elements of their living environment, other friends and neighbors (sometimes far into the past) and even speaking fluently in ancient languages and dialects (with subsequent verification by language scholars) not currently used on this physical plane. Stevenson and colleagues interviewed not only the child and next of kin but also the family of the "reincarnated" deceased person, which often resulted in extraordinarily detailed agreement between the child's story and the story from the other family sometimes hundreds or thousands of miles away. Reviewing the details of individual cases makes it clear that these children are recalling bona fide details of some other existence on this physical plane which they could not in any way have been physically exposed to in their present lifetime. Some have suggested that this proves reincarnation, while others have suggested that the observations can be explained by the idea of so-called nonlocal consciousness, with the brain/consciousness of the present-day child resonating with the consciousness of the deceased individual. IN EITHER CASE, these studies provide strong evidence to suggest that consciousness can and does exist without an intact material brain and that memories are NOT merely stored within a physical brain.

A. THEORY *of* REALITY PRIMARY EVIDENCE

3. Evidence That Brain Activity in and of Itself Cannot Account for Consciousness

1. If brain activity were required for consciousness to exist, we would not be able to exist independently from our bodies and brains, and all of our conscious thoughts and memories would cease to exist following the physical destruction of our brains and bodies (see Primary Evidence #2).

2. Although conventional neurological science has clearly shown that brain function *correlates* with states of consciousness which are in turn *correlated* with various brain structures, there is no evidence that the physical brain is the *source* of consciousness. No specific features or structures of the human brain have been identified as capable of producing consciousness.

3. Wilder Penfield, a Nobel Prize-winning neuroscientist and neurosurgeon, was a revered pioneer in the understanding of the functions of various parts of the human brain. His landmark work, designed in part to prove that the brain accounted for the mind, was extensive and included electrical stimulation

of a wide variety of brain areas among living, awake humans. While stimulation of certain parts of the brain could activate various fragmented memories or streams of memories, Penfield ultimately concluded that "None of the actions that we attribute to the mind has been initiated by electrode stimulation or epileptic discharge.... There is *no* area of grey matter as far as my experience goes, which local epileptic discharge brings to pass what could be called '*mind-action*'...what the mind does is different. It is not to be accounted for by any neuronal mechanism that I can discover.... To expect the highest brain-mechanism or any set of reflexes, however complicated, to carry out what the mind does, and thus perform all the functions of the mind, is quite absurd" (Penfield 1958, 1975). A critical point to consider which Penfield also alluded to is that if the brain generated consciousness, then one would expect that consciousness (or mind action) would be affected by electrical stimulation or seizure activity in some way OTHER than simply being switched off—in other words, other mind-related aspects such as decisions or beliefs would be produced. This simply does not happen.

4. The belief among neuroscientists that consciousness arises from various physical processes within the brain is largely based upon the following types of studies: (1) stimulation studies (such as the electrical stimulation studies mentioned above by Penfield—despite Penfield's ultimate conclusions); (2) ablation studies (part of the brain is damaged or destroyed) and (3) other types of correlation studies involving clinical tests like magnetic resonance imaging (MRI), functional MRI (fMRI), positron emission tomography (PET) scanning or electroencephalography (EEG). In all of these types of studies, the methodology involves determining how a specific area of the physical brain correlates (or is activated

or involved) with a specific aspect of function. However, one can observe that analogous methods are utilized to repair a television set with analogous results—yet this does not warrant the conclusion that the pictures on the screen are coming from within the television set.

5. If our consciousness arose entirely from our brains, then our brain would essentially behave like a materialistic machine controlled by classical physics and chemistry. In such a circumstance, all of our behavior would be the inevitable result of nerve cell activity in the brain and free will would not truly exist. Yet all of us are able to realize that we have the power to decide what we will think about next. It is not up to some material object such as our brain to make that decision for us.

6. There is substantial evidence documenting that our thoughts and other mental processes including emotions, feelings and volition, can change the anatomy and function of the brain at microscopic levels. A recent review article by neuroscientist Mario Beauregard (2007) provided an extensive analysis of the evidence from fMRI and PET scanning performed in conjunction with the intentional repression of emotions (emotional self-regulation), other forms of psychotherapy and placebo treatment. He concluded that mental processes can influence neurophysiological and neurochemical activity in areas of the brain that are involved with pain, movement, perception and various types of emotional processes. An entire body of emerging evidence involving neuroplasticity over the past two decades has clearly shown that focused attention, thought and intention in a wide variety of circumstances can produce substantial and lasting effects upon the physical structures of the brain (Schwartz 2002, Pascual-Leone 2005, Lutz 2007, Begley 2007). Such collective evidence makes it exceedingly unlikely

that consciousness is merely a product or byproduct of the brain or its activity.

7. Despite the human brain having an enormous number of neurons (nerve cells) and synapses (connections between brain nerve cells), there is substantial evidence from the realms of computer science and neuroscience over the past couple of decades presented by Berkovich (1993), Romijn (1997) and others to suggest that the brain's anatomical and functional total storage capacity is incompatible with the possibility of storing of a lifetime of memories. This would suggest that our memories, which are part of the contents of our consciousness (even by materialist definitions), would need to exist outside the realm of physical brain structures.

B. THEORY *of* REALITY SECONDARY EVIDENCE

1. Evidence for Intelligence Outside the Human Brain—Down to the Electron, Photon and C Unit Levels

1. Although the term "intelligence" has been applied by many as a strictly human characteristic, it can be defined in a broader, less human-centric sense as the ability of any being or system to make connections that are meaningful and helpful to that system in its relations with other systems. Hence, any self-organizing system must be imbued with some level of intelligence.

2. Physicians, biologists and microbiologists have come to recognize the enormous complexity and purposeful organizing power of each of the human body's approximately 100 trillion individual cells. Thousands of purposeful, calculated and precise interactions occur every second within each cell in reference to its internal function/survival, as well as its interactions with other cells and the rest of the body and external environment. It is clear that this extraordinary amount and degree of intelligent function, even within one cell (let alone 100 trillion) of our own bodies, is far too complex to be fully understood by the human brain, let alone orchestrated by it.

3. According to systems theory, any self-organizing system must possess some level of intelligence, and various systems at all levels interact with one another to promote life in its various forms at the macro and micro levels. In this way, cells can interact to support more complex systems like bodily organs; which interact to support individual living bodies (e.g., human, animal, plant); which in turn make up villages, herds, forests, etc.; which make up ecosystems; which make up planets and galaxies. Each of these levels has its own intelligence which must continuously allow assessment, interaction and adaptation.

4. The term "mind" in a broader, less human-centric sense can be defined as a pattern of organization that is essential to all living systems. Systems theory recognizes the obvious intelligence extending far beyond individual human and nonhuman minds (which inhabit our body/brain systems without dictating the underlying intelligence of those systems) to the more macro levels of communities, ecosystems, planets and beyond, and to the more micro levels of cells, atoms and subatomic structures. Intelligence derives from the capability of every whole system to make connections with, receive input from and interact with all other related systems and, in this way, to unfold its own inherent potential to serve any and all of the broader wholes.

5. The largest, broadest whole (All That Is)—which includes everything in all dimensions down to the smallest unit of consciousness (and smallest subatomic particles) to the largest universe—is not totally comprehensible to the individual conscious self operating through the human brain (because of conceptual limitations imposed by our brains) but can be intuitively perceived as infinite or divine. The universal intelligence that embraces the entirety of All That Is must exist in all macro and micro levels given the intelligent interconnectedness of all that exists.

6. In each of these systems, including our own bodies, the function, health and survival of the system depends upon constant calculated, purposeful interactions which reflect stunning intelligence. A human, for example, may simultaneously monitor his or her environment for sights, sounds, smells, tastes and other sensations; drive a car down the street; fight off numerous invading infectious bacteria or viruses; isolate and destroy stray toxins or cancer cells; heal a foot sore, hand blister and a cut on the arm; digest food; pump blood through the heart and circulatory system to all organs including the brain; adjust for the effect of gravity when getting out of the car to allow the right amount of blood to be pumped to the brain; constantly regulate the amount of oxygen being extracted from the air and distributed to various parts of the body via the blood; regulate the levels of scores of electrolytes, enzymes and hormones; and, in some cases, even nurture a growing fetus. Such functions (the car notwithstanding) have existed in humans since prehistoric times. They are clearly not being orchestrated by the human mind or brain (nor understood by such) and would be inconceivable without the simultaneous purposeful interaction and cooperation of trillions of unimaginably complex smaller parts of the whole.

7. In the 1940s, the eminent physicist David Bohm produced relevant landmark work on plasmas and electrons within metals while at Berkeley and Princeton. A plasma is a gas-like substance containing a high density of electrons (negatively charged) and positive ions (atoms or molecules with a positive charge). Bohm's observations made clear that once the electrons become involved in a plasma, they stop behaving like individual electrons and start behaving like part of a larger and connected whole. The plasma, like an amoebic organism, continually regenerates itself while enclosing and walling off impurities as a biological organism would wall off foreign substances

in a cyst. This constitutes well-organized cooperation among seas of electrons. Bohm also reported similar behavior among electrons within metals, documenting highly interactive and collaborative efforts among oceans (trillions) of electrons, each behaving as if it knew precisely what the others were doing and precisely how to work within the collective whole (Bohm 1980, 1995).

8. During the course of his career, Einstein revealed that we live in a universe in which energy and matter are so inextricably linked that they cannot be considered separate elements (Einstein 1995). Bohm subsequently demonstrated that EVERYTHING in the universe is part of a single continuum, including space-time (Bohm 1995).

9. In 1982, Alain Aspect and his research team at the University of Paris at Orsay provided experimental evidence to establish unequivocally that photons (light particles) that had been entangled (see point 10 below) were able to react to one another instantaneously regardless of the distance between them with no material exchange of energy. Each particle seemed to know exactly what the other was doing, and the communication between particles 12 meters apart was estimated to occur in about one-billionth of a second, many times faster than the speed at which light would travel in empty space (Aspect 1982).

10. Further experiments such as the one by Bouwmeester et al. in 1997 have also shown the ability of entangled subatomic particles to communicate and respond instantaneously. Entanglement between two or more subatomic particles is generally created by subjecting them to various forms of shared direct interactions. In these experiments, particles were passed through a crystal and thereby entangled prior to being sent in two opposite directions. The first particle then became entangled with a third particle that changed one of the first

particle's characteristics. The second particle then instantaneously received and acted upon the changes that the third particle had passed along to the first particle—again in far less time than it would have taken light to travel between the particles (Bouwmeester 1997).

11. Subsequently, four Swiss physicists from the laboratory of Nicolas Gisin reported an experiment that sent entangled photons (particles of light) along fiber optic cables to different cities which were more than 10 kilometers (6.2 miles) apart (Zbinden 2001). When both photons reached their target cities, they passed through multiple devices that would allow the photons to take one of numerous different paths. Each time, the particles followed the same path as the other, with apparent instantaneous knowledge about which path its entangled twin had taken. The particles were calculated to be in communication about 20,000 times faster than the speed of light, leading the investigators to conclude that "correlations in the quantum world are insensitive to space and time." The distance of more than 10 kilometers (6.2 miles) is extremely vast in the realm of quanta, yet the strength of the correlations did not diminish or weaken over any distance. The results indicate that similar correlations would almost certainly occur even if the particles were billions of miles apart. It is clear that the type of connectedness between and among the involved particles (referred to by Einstein as "spooky action at a distance" long before these experiments were done) is not being transmitted by any conventional means.

12. Consciousness Units (C Units) are the indivisible, fundamental wave equivalents that correspond to various subatomic particles (such as photons) and underlie all particulate structures on this physical plane (see Secondary Evidence #4 and #7). They are different manifestations of the same thing, and the particle version is what we can best see and observe materially. The

C Units are clearly imbued with the same "intelligence" capabilities that transcend this plane of existence. Consciousness and C Units are not directly observable to us within our brains as they constitute the canvas and units of canvas upon which we generate our perceptions rather than the perceptions themselves. On this material plane, we can and do directly observe the particle aspects which correspond to the material manifestations of consciousness and C Units.

13. All of the evidence presented above in this evidence category, along with the evidence presented in each of the other secondary evidence categories, strongly suggests that the universe is a profoundly connected, intelligent, unified living process.

B. THEORY *of* REALITY SECONDARY EVIDENCE

2. Evidence for Coherence and Resonance as Underlying Mechanisms for Communication at Multiple Levels

1. The concepts of coherence and resonance can be demonstrated experimentally in physics and in the biological sciences and are a natural part of all that exists. The term "coherence" implies a certain form of order. In physics, medical sciences and many other fields, coherent *light* is commonly utilized in the form of a laser. Laser light, in contrast to the light we might see from the sun or from an incandescent light bulb, produces light of a single frequency, which makes it possible for laser light to stay in a narrow beam over large distances. Laser (coherent) light is needed to create a hologram (see Secondary Evidence #3).

    Coherent *thought* implies very focused, clean, non-random thought as opposed to disorganized, haphazard, "noisy" thought processes that we are used to in our day-to-day living.

    The term "resonance" relates to the fact that all systems in the universe (from the smallest subatomic particles identifiable, to atoms, all living cells and organisms, planets, stars and galaxies) have a rhythmic oscillation, vibration or frequency.

In music, a string of a violin oscillates or vibrates at a certain frequency (which is within the frequency range that humans can hear as sound). If one places a violin on a table and plays a certain note on another violin across the room, the string that one is playing on the first violin is also humming on the violin on the table. This is an example of resonance (acoustical resonance) between the two violins.

In biological and medical science, all organisms vibrate with characteristic frequencies, and every living cell contains countless vibrating atomic and molecular structures, each with their own specific frequencies. Magnetic resonance imaging (MRI) is an example of a medical test that is based on the phenomenon of resonance as it relates to subatomic (smaller than atoms) structures within the body's cells and tissues, which are subjected to large magnetic fields created by the MRI equipment.

2. The phenomenon of coherence at the subatomic quantum level involving electrons and photons, for example, (see Secondary Evidence #1) has been recognized by Schrödinger, Bohr, Einstein and other physicists since the 1930s. More recent experiments have further informed and refined earlier observations suggesting, among other things, that individual particles have instantaneous connections with each other independent of space and time (Aspect 1982, Bouwmeester 1997, Zbinden 2001), and that individual particles are best characterized not by individual characteristics but rather by the state of the entire ensemble or system in which the particle is embedded (Bohm 1980).

3. In 1995, experiments conducted by physicists Eric Cornell, Wolfgang Ketterle and Carl Wieman (for which they later won the Nobel Prize in 2001) showed that the same phenomenon of coherence that had been observed at the subatomic level also occurs at the macroscopic level. The studies provided con-

clusive evidence that, under certain conditions, large systems of seemingly separate particles behave with remarkable and measurable coherence, whereby separate particles and atomic structures can clearly be shown to interpenetrate as waves (see Secondary Evidence #7 for more on the particle and wave relationships). Such systems have been referred to as Bose-Einstein condensates. The experiments showed, for example, that various types of atoms, such as sodium or rubidium atoms, penetrate as waves throughout the condensate rather than behaving like classical particles (Anderson 1995, Davis 1995).

4. The cells and tissues of living organisms also behave as coherent systems at the macroscopic level as evidenced by the constant plethora of ongoing instantaneous connections that occur throughout the organism. Such connectedness derives from molecules and various molecular assemblies separated by great distances resonating with each other at the same or compatible frequencies. This is the basic mechanism underlying the phenomenon called "macroscopic wave function" of an entire organism, which refers to the instantaneous connection of all parts of an organism (Fröhlich 1968, 1984, 1986; Del Giudice 1982, 1985; Grundler 1983; Penrose 1994; Pokorny 1998; Dürr 2002; Popp 2010).

5. System-wide, quasi-instantaneous communication cannot be accounted for in a human body, for example, by biochemical, electrical or other physical interactions (which are commonly recognized in the materialistic aspects of medical and neurological science) among genes, cells or organ systems. Biochemical signaling is fairly slow, and electrical conduction through the nervous system is about 50 meters per second. Such mechanisms cannot even begin to account for the speed, diversity and multidimensionality of coherence and communication that occurs in the human body and other living organisms (see Secondary Evidence #1).

6. Every cell in a human body (approximately 100 trillion) takes part in many thousands of biochemical reactions every second, meaning that many thousands of trillions of signals are constantly taking place. The coherent instantaneous behavior of these cells as part of tissues and organ systems in the second-to-second function (let alone function over days or years) of one's body is beyond the capability of the human brain to fully comprehend. Chemical and electrical reaction sequences alone are FAR too slow and inefficient to even begin to account for all of the signals and exchanges of information that must occur on an ongoing basis.

7. Some of the most incredible evidence in support of *cosmic* coherence can be found when one looks at the almost unimaginable fine tuning of the universe that we generally take for granted (Barrow 1986, Kafatos 2000). Scientists have examined dozens of factors and have concluded that even minor deviations in at least 30 basic parameters would have an enormous impact on the viability of the universe and its inhabitants. Physicists and astronomers have calculated, for example, that minimal changes (variance by one-millionth of a percent) in the strength of electromagnetic vs. gravitational fields would have prevented the formation of stable hot stars like our sun, which would have in turn prevented the existence of surrounding planets such as the earth along with all of its life forms. Other physicists and chemists have pointed out that even minimal changes in the electrical charges of protons and electrons, or minimal changes in the precise masses of protons and neutrons relative to electrons (which make up atoms), would have precluded most chemical reactions and rendered all configurations of matter unstable, leaving the universe as a mixture of gases and various types of radiation. On the basis of a variety of these parameters, the eminent mathematical physicist Roger

Penrose from Oxford has calculated that the probability of our universe occurring by random selection is approximately 1 in 1 followed by 10 to the 123rd power of successive zeros. For reference, 10 to the 9th power is equal to one billion, so Penrose's number would be 1 followed by unimaginably more than a billion zeros (Penrose 1989). This amount of precision or coherence relative to our universe is truly unimaginable and would obviously not have occurred by chance.

8. In 2007, Engel et al., in an article in the journal *Nature*, provided evidence for coherence at the quantum level in plants involving the process of photosynthesis. In this process, the authors documented the conversion of the sun's energy (in the form of photon light particles) into chemical energy via a form of "wavelike energy transfer" resulting from coherent oscillations in both donor and acceptor molecules. In other words, the wave aspects of the sun's photon particles *resonated* with the wave aspects of molecular particles in the plant, producing an information/energy transfer (Engel 2007).

9. More recently, Persinger et al. (Persinger 2008) have provided detailed calculations to suggest that individual human brain cell membranes (outer coverings) have specific characteristics and dimensions that make them resonant with all space within the material universe that we can observe. The authors concluded that their calculations suggested that human thought, as a wave form associated with brain cell activity (see Secondary Evidence #7), has the potential to affect any or all matter in the known universe via resonance and entanglement (see Secondary Evidence #1, #4 and #7).

10. Further research from several investigators including Matsukevich et al. (2004) and Chaneliere et al. (2005) has documented under carefully controlled laboratory conditions the transfer of information between light and matter through the phenomenon

of resonance—more precisely, nuclear spin resonance, and electron spin resonance referring to correlation of the wave aspects of photons (light particles) with the wave aspects of nuclei and electrons (contained within atoms of matter). A similar form of information transfer occurs between the C Field (an underlying universal consciousness/information field as described in Secondary Evidence #4) and the physical brain.

B. THEORY *of* REALITY SECONDARY EVIDENCE

3. Evidence for a Holographic Type of Organization Underlying Our Brains and Our Universe

1. It is useful and relevant to begin this section by reviewing some of the principles underlying the hologram. Dennis Gabor (1900–1979) was awarded the Nobel Prize in Physics in 1971 for his discovery of holography in 1947. He coined the term hologram from the Greek words *holos* meaning "whole" and *gramma* meaning "message." Simply stated, holography is the process of capturing three-dimensional images by recording patterns of light wave reflections.

   A hologram can be created by splitting a beam of laser (coherent) light (see Secondary Evidence #2) in two, bouncing one of the resulting two beams (the object beam) off an object such as a clock (**figure 1**) and simply directing the other beam (the reference beam) to recombine with the object beam, producing interference patterns on a piece of film.

   The interference patterns are created by the waves of light intersecting with each other (in much the same way as throwing a couple of pebbles in still water will create waves that intersect

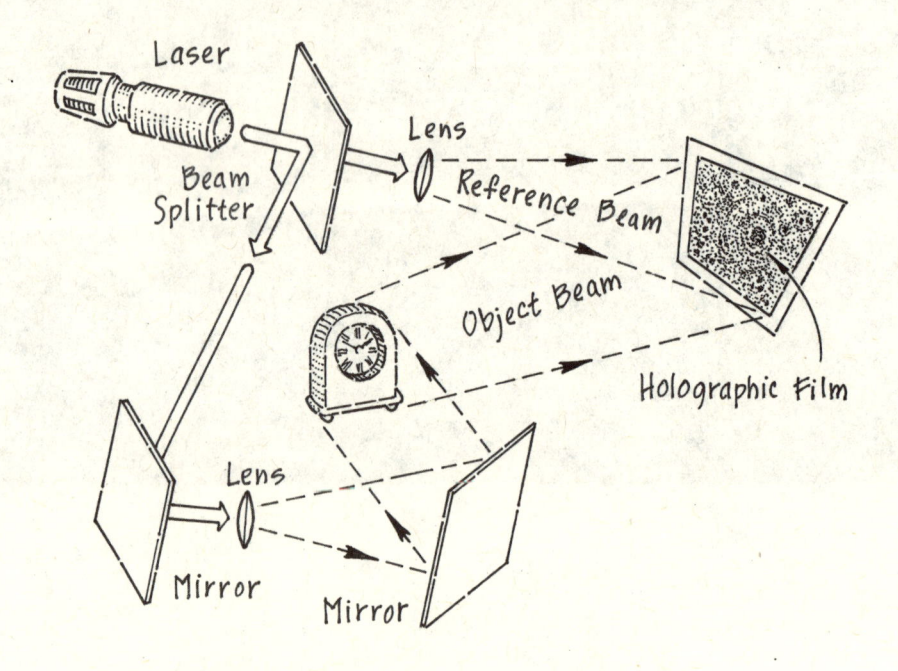

Figure 1. Holographic Film Exposure Process

with each other and create their own interference patterns). [*Note*: If one were to freeze the water and look at the arcs of the waves created by the pebbles and how they intersect, one could trace back and know the location, shape and size of the pebbles and when they hit the water—in other words, information has been stored regarding the event of the pebbles hitting the water and their characteristics.] On the piece of holographic film, the interference patterns don't look anything like the original object but rather like a hodgepodge of irregular ripples (**figure 2**).

By shining another beam of laser light similar to the reference beam through the piece of film, one is able to view a three-dimensional image (visual hologram) of the object (**figure 3**). One can walk all the way around the projected image and view

Theory of Reality Secondary Evidence #3 59

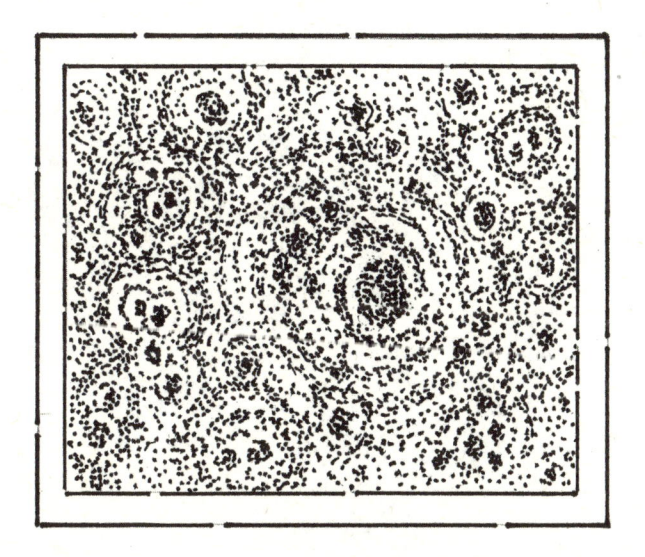

Figure 2. Holographic Film Interference Patterns

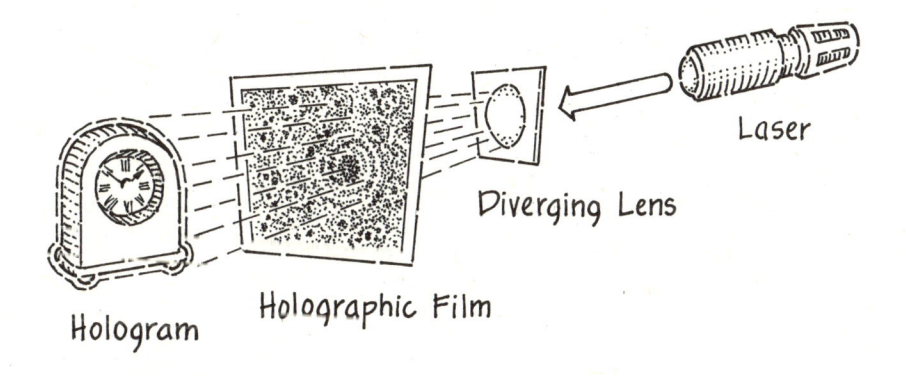

Figure 3. Creation of 3D Holographic Image

it from above and below as one would a real object—but if one reaches out to touch it, one's hand will go right through it.

A remarkable and very important feature of the hologram is that if a piece of the holographic film is cut in half (or into

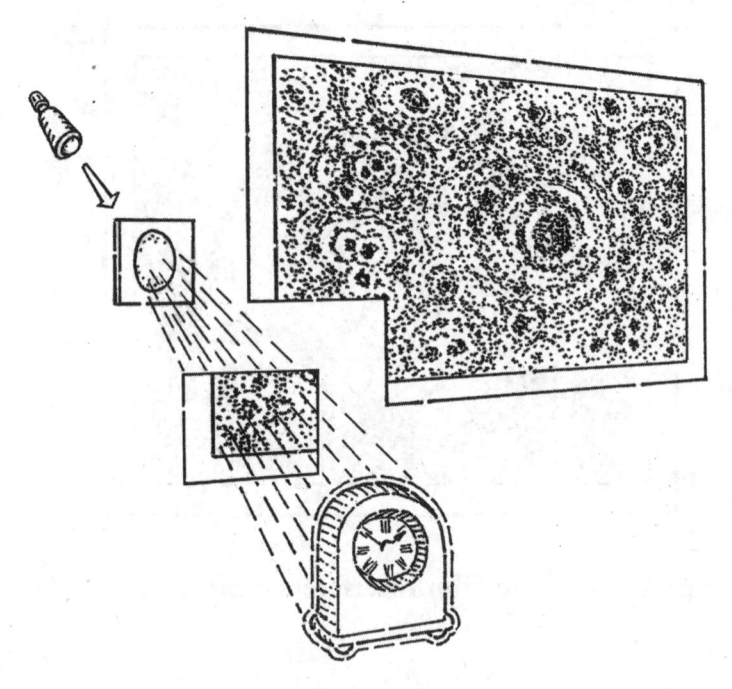

Figure 4. Illuminating a Fragment of Holographic Film with Coherent Light Produces a Whole Object

smaller and smaller fragments) EVERY fragment can produce a WHOLE OBJECT when illuminated with a laser (coherent) light (**figure 4**). In other words, every piece contains the whole.

In these examples, the holographic mechanism has stored information (which could later be retrieved) from the interference patterns of waves regarding the appearance of the object (a clock in **figure 1**) on the holographic film and regarding the pebbles hitting the water. Since all that exists (from the smallest identifiable particles in physics to the largest galaxy—see Secondary Evidence #2, #4 and #7) and all that we experience in our lifetimes (including perceptions, thoughts and activities) are associated with the production of wave components (e.g., vibrations), the holographic principle can act as nature's information storage device for all that happens in the universe when coupled with a field such as the C Field (see Secondary Evidence #4).

The critical part of a holographic image is the interaction of a *reference beam* (coherent, virgin, untouched beam) with a *working beam*, which has had some experiences (interactions). Our whole reality is constructed from constantly making such comparisons, not just through sight but via all our senses. We don't have an *absolute* reference for our senses, but each of them generates their own.

2. On the basis of a typical materialistic model, the brain's anatomic and functional storage capacity is incompatible with the possibility of storing a lifetime of memories and information (see Primary Evidence #3). An underlying holographic information storage mechanism opens up the possibility of an enormously extended capacity which is needed to explain empiric observations in this realm.

3. Neurosurgeon/neuroscientist Karl Pribram from Yale and Stanford has made numerous fundamental contributions in the areas of cognitive function, memory and brain topography. He and physicist David Bohm from the University of London are widely credited with initially describing how the concepts and ideas of Dennis Gabor regarding holography can be applied to the underlying organization and function of the brain and the broader universe (Pribram 1977, Bohm 1980).

4. One of the things that Pribram and others had noted was that memory seemed to be distributed throughout the brain and that traces of the same memory could be elicited from stimuli in multiple areas of the brain. Furthermore, following brain injuries or even removal of large parts of the brain, discrete chunks of memory were not lost. Although neurophysiologists had long thought that memories might be laid down in bits as "engrams" at specific locations in the brain, with changes in brains cells marking such memory traces, no such organization

was ever found. In contrast to the engram concept (and others that have been proposed), a holographic organizing principle for memory storage fits with the empiric observations regarding the effects of injury, disease and surgical alteration of the brain.

5. An underlying holographic organization to the motor system can explain how motor skills can be transferred from one limb to another. For instance, even if one is right handed, one can usually write with one's left hand or with one's right foot or even while holding a pencil in one's teeth. The part of the brain that controls the left hand or the right foot or the teeth has not generally written anything before, yet those groups of cells are able to process information about writing and utilize it to write. This would NOT be possible if the brain were hard wired with fixed connections between parts as has generally been assumed.

6. A related feature of our perceptive capabilities also speaks strongly against our brains being hard wired. This involves our ability to recognize an object, such as a familiar face, regardless of the distance or the perspective from which it is viewed. In other words, regardless of how near or far across a room a friend is sitting, for example, one can recognize the friend's face, and it doesn't seem as if the friend's head has enlarged or shrunk. Such transposition capabilities are much more compatible with an underlying holographic organization than with materialistic hard wiring.

7. An underlying holographic organization to our senses and memories can also account for the nature of our associative memory functions. Anyone can identify with the way that a particular smell of a food being prepared or the sound of a song or gazing upon a long-forgotten object can cause one to be suddenly flooded with constellations of memories out of the past and can take one to specific scenes and moments. Many times,

exposure to some sight or sound or smell will initially leave one with a vague feeling of deeper personal significance or déjà vu, and later the entire memory association will become apparent. It is relevant to note that when visual holograms are created by bouncing a laser light off two objects simultaneously, as one might expect, illuminating *either* of the objects with laser light will also create a hologram of the other.

8. Fourier transforms (discovered in the 18th century by Jean B. J. Fourier) represent a form of mathematical equation that Gabor used to create the first holograms. A Fourier analysis represents a form of calculus that transforms any complex pattern into its simplified component sine waves. Helmholtz described how this kind of analysis could explain the functioning of the human auditory system (Cahan 1994), and Bernstein later applied the same analyses to the motor system (Bernstein 1967). Bernstein dressed individuals in black leotards with white dots painted at the locations of their joints and took movies of them dancing (or doing other activities such as hammering nails) against black backgrounds. What resulted was white dots moving up and down along the film creating *wave forms* (**figure 5**). It became clear that any motor movement could be reduced to wave forms and converted back to the actual movements utilizing Fourier transforms. In the late 1960s, Fergus Campbell at Cambridge showed that the visual system also worked as a frequency (wave form) analyzer for patterns rather than primarily as a "feature analyzer" as had been widely assumed (Campbell 1968). Subsequently, in 1979, Russell and Karen DeValois at Berkeley performed a landmark experiment in which they mathematically converted a plaid pattern into the Fourier domain by computer and found that the cells of the visual cortex of the brain *responded to the Fourier transform of the plaid and NOT to the plaid itself* (DeValois

Figure 5. Illustration of Bernstein's Experiment Converting Dance Movement to Wave Forms

1979). This crucial finding has subsequently been verified by numerous other laboratories.

9. That the visual system analyzes patterns into their component frequencies and composes visual memories from wave forms organized in holographic form accounts for phenomena like imitative learning. It would be unimaginably difficult to learn how to hit a baseball or kick a soccer ball by watching others if one had to extract every feature of what one was copying and describe every component of every move, feature by feature. One does not think through how to imitate every feature of every instant of a process. Instead one simply watches the activity and goes out and tries it. Since the brain can analyze and convert the activity into its component wave forms, it can activate the appropriate holographic motor pattern and allow the entire movement to be readily approximated without thinking about it.

10. In a computer, transforming data into the Fourier domain allows a quantum jump in the speed of data analysis. There is a parallel between this type of holographic computer organization and the way our brains rapidly process information, make correlations and make decisions. For example, when one is rapidly analyzing one's immediate environment in a room filled with several people (some of whom one has met and had experiences with and some not), while simultaneously contemplating a complex situation and goals that need to be accomplished, one doesn't have to think things through in 1-2-3 step sequences (one step at a time). Rather, the brain's holographic form of organization allows one to take in the whole constellation of the situation, immediately analyze correlations, isolate critical components and make decisions on multiple levels at the same time.

11. All of this is not to say that the brain IS a hologram, nor to imply that its organizational pattern could be cast in the form of a single holographic pattern. (For example, there is evidence in the visual system that a single cell has a receptive field that covers about 5 degrees of a visual angle, meaning that one's entire visual receptive field would need to involve a vast collection of holographically organized patches). Rather, the hologram itself and the principles behind it turn out to be the best way at this point for us (functioning within our brains on this material plane) to understand and approximate the concept of nonlocal information storage and retrieval where memory is instantaneously and nonlocally accessible, and all other sensory (visual, auditory, tactile, smell, taste) information is nonlocal as well.

12. The life review part of Near-Death Experiences (see Primary Evidence #1) has a number of holographic features, including the three-dimensional panoramic aspects, the incredible display of information storage capacity, the instantaneous reliving of every thought and emotion associated with one's life's

experiences along with the associated emotions of others who were impacted by those experiences, and the ability to *simultaneously comprehend the whole in every part* as part of the process.

13. We see further evidence of holographic principles outside our brains. Every cell in a human or nonhuman body contains all the information needed to create an entire duplicate body mirroring the holographic principle noted above—namely that every piece contains the information of the whole.

14. The broader universe at both the micro and macro levels is a fully connected, coherent living process (see Secondary Evidence #1, #2 and #4). As such, things that appear to be separated from each other can, nonetheless, be in instant communication and information contained within the C Field is universally and instantaneously available (see Secondary Evidence #4). As in a visual hologram, the interfering wave fields that emanate from all that exists and that record an infinitesimal amount of information in the form of interference patterns are natural cosmic holograms. Nature's cosmic holograms thus inform and connect all things with all other things. This sharing of information down to the granular level is nature's way of increasing the likelihood of survival of the biosphere and the cosmos.

15. On a more practical level, we can see holographic principles being utilized in many places in the world around us, all the way from credit card holographic images as a means of enhancing security to holographic disc (HVD) and computer data storage (which many project to revolutionize disc and computer data storage and transfer) to the medical imaging techniques of magnetic resonance imaging (MRI) and functional MRI which, as with a quantum hologram, incorporate non-

local information exchange at the subatomic level (see Secondary Evidence #2).

16. Again, none of the above should be construed to infer that the universe IS all a hologram but rather that it is organized in many *facets* using many of the same *principles* as those which underlie the hologram.

B. THEORY *of* REALITY SECONDARY EVIDENCE

4. Evidence for a C Field as a Basic Underlying Matrix or Fabric for Reality (as We Experience It Here and in Other Dimensions) and for Some Unit of This Fabric (C Unit) as the Most Fundamental Building Block of the Universe

1. On the basis of a lifetime of research and landmark contributions in physics, Einstein proposed that reality consists of fields and that particles are regions within these fields. Every type of matter that we perceive on this plane is a collection of electrical charges interacting across a diverse background of electromagnetic and other energy fields. The principles of quantum physics suggest that the universe as we observe it from this plane consists of an amalgamation of these interdependent energy fields.

2. Energy and associated energy fields are particle aspects that we can generally see and measure on this plane of existence. All energy and matter have more generative manifestations that underlie them arising ultimately from pure consciousness. Alain Aspect's work in the 1980s (see Secondary Evidence #1) showed that photons (light particles) instantaneously register and act upon each other's situation without regard to time or distance, documenting that in our

usual way of materially perceiving things, the photons no longer had any location and that it was meaningless to think of them as separate. From this and other confirmatory work, it follows that the basic essence of all matter and energy exists as components of one deeper and fundamental unity which includes everything that is.

3. Consciousness *contains* all matter and the world/universe. It is the canvas upon which our impressions are generated and is a wave manifestation (as opposed to a particle manifestation) which is why we don't see consciousness "out there" with other particle manifestations of matter on this physical plane. It is the creative canvas for our thoughts as well as for all matter that we experience here, and its wave character is compatible with other deeper dimensions that underlie this plane (see Secondary Evidence #6 and #7). It follows that a unit of consciousness would be the basic building block for everything in this as well as deeper dimensions.

4. The evidence for an underlying C Field that would generate, connect, inform and guide all that exists is not direct (on this material plane) but rather must be constructed from what we can perceive while in these bodies and brains. As is the case with many fields well known to modern physics, including the electromagnetic field, the gravitational field and various quantum fields, the C Field cannot be perceived with our senses and hence cannot be touched, seen, heard, smelled or tasted. Yet these fields all produce EFFECTS that we CAN perceive. The electromagnetic field is experienced through its making possible the transmission of electrical and magnetic forces. Similarly, the gravitational field is experienced not directly through our senses but through observing an object drop to the ground at a specific speed rather than float off into space. The C Field produces effects that include the instantaneous (well beyond any speed that we can accurately measure and at least 20,000

times the speed of light) connecting, informing and guiding of all that exists down to the smallest particles that we can measure. We can also perceive the effects of the generative (creative) aspect of the C Field perhaps most directly in the form of our thoughts that are created from consciousness.

5. Max Planck, widely considered to be the founder of modern quantum physics, at least partly envisioned consciousness as the essence of a field or matrix which underlies all matter when he declared in a speech in 1944, "As a man who has devoted his whole life to the most clear-headed science, to the study of matter, I can tell you as a result of my research about atoms this much: There is no matter as such! All matter originates and exists only by virtue of a force which brings the particles of an atom to vibration and holds this most minute solar system together.... We must assume behind this force the existence of a conscious and intelligent mind. This mind is the matrix of all matter." In a prior interview, Planck had also indicated, "I regard consciousness as fundamental. I regard matter as derivative from consciousness. We cannot get behind consciousness. Everything that we regard as existing, postulates consciousness."

6. Over the past several decades, a multitude of published scientific experiments have documented and replicated evidence that the type of nonlocal "entanglement" previously described by Alain Aspect and others regarding subatomic particles in physics (see Secondary Evidence #1) also applies to human consciousness and biological systems at the macroscopic level (Duane 1965, Targ 1974; Puthoff 1976; Wackermann 2003; Standish 2003, 2004; Radin 2004; Pizzi 2004; Acterberg 2005; Richards 2005, Persinger 2010). Studies have included monitoring of highly "connected" individuals (such as family members or others who feel very close to one another) as well as individuals and their therapists with electroencephalography (EEG) and imaging studies such as functional magnetic resonance

imaging (fMRI). These studies have documented instantaneous transfer of information between individuals with, for example, one individual being stimulated by flashing lights and manifesting the expected EEG changes, and the other at a great distance in an isolated Faraday chamber within a separate laboratory instantaneously manifesting synchronized changes in their EEG patterns despite no light stimulation whatsoever. Since the Faraday chamber precludes all electronic and magnetic energy transfer, the information exchange cannot be explained by classical scientific fields or models.

7. The same sorts of phenomena involving nonlocal connectedness and/or quasi-instantaneous coherent communication have been documented among nonhuman animals and *between* humans and nonhumans, including numerous carefully documented observations and experiments with primates, with dogs, cats and other companion animals; and with other species such as birds and rabbits (McFarland 1982; Sheldrake 1995, 1998, 2011; Peoc'h 1997; Long 2005; Cavagna 2010).

8. The ongoing, quasi-instantaneous coherent communication that exists within cells and within entire organisms such as human and nonhuman bodies (see Secondary Evidence #2) has been well documented and cannot be accounted for on the basis of biochemical, electrical or other physical interactions (Pokorny 1998, Bishof 2000, Dürr 2002).

9. In a detailed series of studies, Cleve Backster et al. documented that an individual's living cells continue to be affected by that individual's thoughts and emotions after the cells are removed from the individual's body. The cells manifested strong changes in electrical potentials instantaneously when the donor was subjected to strong emotional stimuli (and consequently experienced emotional peaks and dips) at distances of up to 50 miles away (Backster 1985).

10. More recently, Dotta et al. documented that when two aggregates of genetically similar cells from humans or nonhumans are induced to be coherent (and thereby entangled) by simultaneous application of certain types of external magnetic fields, light flashes delivered to one aggregate of cells instantaneously evoked increased photon (light particle) emission from another aggregate of cells maintained in a separate dark room. The authors concluded that their results support accumulating evidence for "intercellular and interbrain communications with potential quantum-like properties" (Dotta 2011).

11. The informing (or information) aspect of the C Field (which goes hand in hand with the guidance aspect) is a fundamental aspect of nature and is present in the world independent of human thought and action. The eminent physicist David Bohm clearly recognized this aspect at all levels in the physical sciences and labeled it "in-formation," suggesting a process that actually "forms" the recipient. Other evidence for this aspect can clearly be found in the biological and cosmological sciences. The C Field is the holographically organized (see Secondary Evidence #3) information storage mechanism that not only records all of the historical experience of matter but can also convey it to any form of "resonant" (see Secondary Evidence #2) receiver, including subatomic particles, atoms molecules, cells, whole organisms, populations, ecologies, planets and beyond. Scientists and systems theorists such as Gazdag and Laszlo have delineated the theoretical basis for the process of wave formation and wave memory via the meeting of wave fields and the creation of wave interference patterns as they relate to any micro or macro physical structure (Gazdag 1998, Laszlo 2003). In this format, there is no limit to the amount of information that could be conserved, meaning that such a mechanism could carry information on the state of the entire universe.

12. The information storage and exchange mediated by the C Field can be further illustrated in the coherence of living organisms (see Secondary Evidence #2 for more on this). Within living organisms, one can witness tens of thousands of genes, billions of protein molecules that make up a cell, and the many kinds of cells making up tissues and organs, all of which engage in quasi-instantaneous system wide assessments, responses and modifications in countless directions simultaneously to simply *maintain* the organism, let alone to accomplish extraordinarily complex activities. The massive amounts of information involved are way beyond the scope of what can be fully comprehended or understood, let alone orchestrated by the human brain. However, the almost unimaginable mass of ongoing information doesn't overload or clog up the human brain because the brain limits our capacity to resonate at all of these levels. Karl Pribram, the eminent neuroscientist, has previously suggested that the brain has a mechanism to limit such masses of information which would otherwise overload the human brain and our thought processes (Pribram 1977).

13. All of the evidence delineated in points 6 through 11 above, (and augmented by Secondary Evidence categories #1, #2, #3, #6, and #7) suggests an underlying connective field or matrix which links consciousness, thought, cells, biological systems and the rest of the physical world.

14. Numerous individuals reporting NDEs have experienced a life review which they consistently describe as an instantaneous process involving incredibly vivid three-dimensional wrap-around depictions of every moment from every year of their life, which is played back in full sensory detail and includes the element of how others felt as well as how they themselves felt. Such experiences provide insight into the enormous information storage capacity which is not occurring within a human brain (see Primary Evidence #1 and the NDE part of the Tools

and Techniques section regarding the nature of NDEs, and Primary Evidence #3 regarding brain memory storage), suggesting the need for another information storage mechanism (such as the C Field). Given that the information is recorded and played back independent of space and time, such a mechanism must have a derivation deeper than this plane of existence.

15. Another aspect of numerous documented NDEs and other Peak Experiences (see Secondary Evidence #5 point 4 and Primary Evidence #1) has included individuals experiencing another realm or level of existence in which they have had access to the sum total of all knowledge existing in a sort of timeless state encompassing past, present and future. The storage of such universal knowledge (or information) is clearly not occurring within one's brain or any other material structure and must reside within a wave-based deeper reality (see Secondary Evidence #6) with nonlocal (independent of time and space) characteristics capable of connecting, informing and guiding everything in the universe. Such features are consistent with and strongly suggestive of a fundamental universal underlying C Field.

16. The particle and wave aspects that coexist within all matter and energy, including those aspects and effects that we can perceive with our materially oriented senses, have been repeatedly observed over the past century and are now widely accepted by essentially all of mainstream physics (see Secondary Evidence #7). Without a truly fundamental C Field, these particle and wave aspects and effects which we observe would not have a clear mechanism for actualization (creation, sustenance and annihilation); information sharing; connecting; and organizing into relatively stable forms at all levels. The eminent physicist David Bohm and others have produced detailed analyses which demonstrate from the perspectives of physics and mathematics

substantial evidence for a deeper organizing and informing universal wave function (Bohm 1995, Li 1995, Nichol 2003).

17. Quantum physicists have conclusively shown that at the subatomic (smaller than atoms) level of virtual particles, "things" don't exist in material form but rather as fleeting displays of tendencies and superimposed possibilities with nonlocality and indeterminacy. This is also the nature of consciousness as we experience it. Given that the universe is incredibly interactive and coherent at all levels (see Secondary Evidence #1 and #2), it is inconceivable that individual consciousness would be fundamentally different than the essential nature of the rest of the cosmos and still be connected with it in the ways we can observe. It follows that consciousness is the most fundamental fabric of the universe, the essence of which constitutes a fine structural field (C Field) that pervades all that exists.

B. THEORY *of* REALITY SECONDARY EVIDENCE

5. Evidence for Various Types of Peak Experiences and Other Related Phenomena Being Associated with Discoveries, Creativity, and Other Types of Uncommon Insight and Understanding

1. Peak Experiences (PEs) encompass a range of phenomena [Abraham Maslow (1994), Colin Wilson (2009) and others have written extensively about them] which generally involve seconds to minutes in which one feels the highest levels of peace, connectedness, happiness, harmony and possibility. They often are pivotal moments in a person's life and are often associated with key insights, "waves of understanding," and/or "thought balls," which are generally integrative in nature (a sense of meaning comes from finding a form of unity and from putting the right things together in the right order). They occur in science, the arts and all forms of creativity, and to some extent have been associated with various landscapes, events, locations, art forms, other human and nonhuman beings and a wide range of techniques and triggers.

2. A variety of other related phenomena have been associated with producing or facilitating Peak Experiences or with otherwise deeply enhancing one's creative, intellectual, visionary

or integrative understanding and/or capabilities. Among these phenomena are Near Death Experiences (NDEs), Out-of-Body Experiences (OOBEs), various types of yoga and meditation, intentional techniques to connect with one's "higher self," and numerous other spiritual, metaphysical and/or religious practices.

3. Einstein observed, "The intellect has little to do on the road to discovery. There comes a leap in consciousness, call it intuition or what you will, and the solution comes to you and you don't know how or why." Nobel laureate Louis de Broglie commented, "The great epoch-making discoveries in the history of science (think, for example, of that of universal gravitation) have been like sudden lightning flashes, making us perceive in one single glance a harmony up till then unsuspected...." Similar descriptions have been offered by countless scientists, artists, musicians and others who have been involved in extraordinary discoveries and/or have demonstrated uncommon creativity, insight and/or understanding which often seems to come in the form of instantaneous packages of ideas (thought balls) and seems to be drawn from some form of connection between one's consciousness and a different (higher) level. This "level" is entirely consistent with a deeper/finer/higher level underlying this physical plane connected to anyone and anything via nonlocal space and the C Field (see Secondary Evidence #4, #6 and #7).

4. As a part of several studies involving NDEs, numerous individuals have reported experiencing a separate realm or level of existence in which the individual had access to all knowledge which seemed to coexist in a sort of timeless state encompassing past, present and future. Similar experiences (often reported as relatively brief glimpses) have occasionally been reported by individuals as part of various other types of Peak Experiences, including OOBEs and other meditative/intentional

experiences. Even the most fulminate of these experiences (which have been reported in connection with NDEs) have not resulted in retention of the feelings of complete knowledge once an individual has returned to "normal" functioning within his or her body and brain. Yet the experience, while generally beyond words and difficult to describe in our usual language, has, in many cases, had a profound and lasting beneficial effect (e.g., enhanced intuitive capabilities, uncommon understanding) on the individual (see Primary Evidence #1). Such experiences are consistent with the need to be (at least somewhat) free of one's brain (and one's materialistic brain processes) in order to access these types of experiences. They also reflect some of the brain's limiting or filtering functions which are commensurate with this physical materialistic plane. The "universal knowledge" component would clearly be expected to "reside" in connection with nonlocal space and the C Field (see Primary Evidence #3, and Secondary Evidence #3, #4, #6, #7 and #8).

5. When one considers the various techniques that have been associated with producing or facilitating Peak Experiences or other insights, creativity and/or uncommon understanding, the elements that they have in common include: focused attention, deep relaxation, and getting one's consciousness free from the endless stream of "waking chatter" and the "noise" of day-to-day living. These elements clearly enhance one's coherence (see Secondary Evidence #2), and a coherent consciousness appears to be of fundamental importance to tapping into normally subconscious or latent abilities as well as accessing various levels and types of information enfolded within the C Field and nonlocal space (see Secondary Evidence #2, #3, #4 and #6).

6. It is also important to recognize that increasing one's coherence does not necessarily require accomplishing any particular

"difficult" technique or austere lifestyle—or a specifically prescribed altered state of consciousness or OOBE. In general, factors that increase one's *resilience* and *equanimity* also tend to increase one's coherence. *Resilience* is the capacity following adverse or stressful events to adapt to (and even thrive in) the resulting challenges and changing circumstances. Such a capacity proactively insulates and protects individuals from a variety of anxiety disorders and depression. Similarly, *equanimity* is the inner strength and stability to experience well-being and confidence in the *eye of the storm*—enabling one to maintain a relaxed body and calm, balanced mind regardless of the circumstances. It allows one to remain centered and to see the big picture with perspective and patience. Factors that are generally enjoyable for individuals which increase one's resilience and equanimity include laughter, music, intimacy (including friendship and sexual intimacy), spiritual exploration and understanding, and sleep. There is considerable evidence to suggest that enhancing these factors, which are normally fun and compelling in themselves, can increase one's coherence while optimizing brain and neurological function as well as psychological health (Ornish 1998, Wiebers 2001, Seligman 2002).

7. Even modest increases in one's coherence can have clear benefits in one's day-to-day life on this physical plane and would be expected to make it more likely for one to experience various forms of Peak Experiences, enhanced creativity, insights, etc. More substantial increases in coherence, even for short periods (which may or may not be associated with or precipitated by certain intentional phenomena/techniques/practices as mentioned above), can clearly facilitate PEs, uncommon understanding, discoveries, insights, enhanced creativity etc. Therefore, the potential value of increasing one's coherence (by whatever methods resonate with the individual) becomes self-evident.

8. Although much effort has been expended in trying to study the nature of Peak Experiences and other related phenomena with materialistic scientific methods and, on this basis, to attempt to conclude that the phenomena are either "real" or not, most of the essence of these phenomena is clearly beyond the realm of what conventional science (as we currently construct it) can address. As with other wave (nonmaterial) phenomena, we are unable to directly see or measure the phenomena themselves, only certain limited material effects associated with them (see Secondary Evidence #7). While some will insist that there can be no value or reality in anything that materialistic science cannot currently directly measure, it is clear that such an approach is open only to a very miniscule fraction of what exists in the universe (see Secondary Evidence #8) and that taking such an approach subjects one to missing or ignoring some of the most important aspects of existence.

9. In the end, the most compelling evidence regarding the value of such phenomena will not come from whether or not materialistic science can somehow measure or account for them, but rather from the benefit or lack thereof of these phenomena to the individuals who experience them and to others whom the individual can subsequently help.

10. NDEs have been systematically studied more than any of the other techniques in this regard, and although there are arguable shortcomings associated with many of these studies, there now exists a considerable body of evidence documenting that NDEs commonly and profoundly change individuals for the better for the rest of their lives on this plane. These changes include: decreased fear of death and dying; increased compassion and tolerance for others; increased thirst for knowledge; enhanced appreciation for life; greater interest in spirituality (and less interest in specific religious affiliation); greater sense of social justice; enhanced intuitive capabilities (precognition,

telepathy, intuition, perceptive abilities); greater understanding of the purpose of life; and a heightened sense of self-worth (Ring 1998, Lommel 2010).

11. Studies of other various phenomena and techniques are limited but have generally suggested positive impacts. For example, studies of individuals participating in programs (designed to focus consciousness and/or facilitate OOBEs) at the Monroe Institute have suggested benefits in the realms of self-efficacy (e.g., greater understanding of life, clearer sense of purpose, enhanced ability to resolve important issues or challenges) and life satisfaction (Danielson 2010).

12. Ultimately, the value of these phenomena and experiences comes down to a very individual and personal level as it should. From the time that humans are born on this planet, they are taught to look outward and look to various institutions—academic institutions, economic institutions, political institutions, social institutions, etc.—for meaning and for answers. In reality, they need to look inward for answers. Everything that is needed is inward. The JOURNEY itself (and active participation as opposed to passive acceptance) is of great importance. As Einstein observed, "The pursuit of knowledge is more valuable than its possession."

B. THEORY *of* REALITY SECONDARY EVIDENCE

6. Evidence for Other "Finer" Levels of Existence Enfolded into the Same Space and Time as This Physical Plane

1. There is considerable scientific evidence that the material (physical) universe that we perceive around us constitutes only a miniscule portion of all that exists (see Secondary Evidence #8). Moreover, physics tells us that the vast majority of the energy that we are missing and are unable to access resides in the higher frequencies (see Secondary Evidence #8) where energy densities are greater than what we generally deal with in our day-to-day lives on this physical plane—and much greater than the densities of our bodies or even substances such as lead which we consider to be very dense. Together, these factors strongly suggest that what we are currently missing in our materialist perception of reality must involve other dimensions at higher (finer) frequencies. That we cannot readily "tune in" to these higher frequencies needn't come as a great surprise to us given that our brains are a form of transducer which is constantly converting wave-form information into particle-type information and often "stepping down" frequencies in the

process (see Secondary Evidence #2, #3, #4, #7). It is analogous to tuning into the right frequency ("being on the same wavelength") to listen to a particular radio or television station—when we (or the transducer we are using) are not on the same wavelength or frequency, we can't perceive the station even though it is there around us in what appears to be "empty space." Again, the station exists in the same space and time, yet if we're not tuned in, we don't perceive it. Obviously, if we did not have any transducer or filter and were tuned into all frequencies (including all TV and radio stations in all languages on earth, as a modest example) at once, it would be more than a minor overload in terms of our processing capabilities.

2. David Bohm is widely considered to be one of the most significant quantum physicists of all time based upon decades of work and landmark publications involving numerous areas, including the experimental documentation of the striking interconnectedness of subatomic particles regardless of the distance between them (the phenomena of entanglement and nonlocality) and the particle-wave aspects of a variety of forms of matter and energy. He is also widely credited with being the first physicist to clearly propose that the physical or "particle" manifestations that we perceive here in this physical dimension (which he refers to as the "explicate" or "unfolded" order) all have corresponding "wave" manifestations in a deeper level of reality (which he refers to as the "implicate" or "enfolded" order). He proposed that the ongoing and flowing exchange between the two orders explains how particles such as electrons or photons (particles of light) can manifest as either particles or waves. He also proposed that a holographically organized deeper order accounts for everything becoming nonlocal (location no longer exists as we know it on this plane) at the subatomic level, using the analogy of a piece of holographic film containing all of the information of the whole (see Secondary

Evidence #3) as a form of nonlocal information distribution, whereby the whole is distributed everywhere (Bohm 1980, 1995). This form of organization is consistent with a universe that is a unified living process rather than a collection of separate objects.

3. Landmark experimental neuroscience studies by Russell and Karen DeValois at Berkeley in 1979 (which have subsequently been confirmed by many other laboratories) provided compelling evidence that the brain does not respond to material features but rather to wave or frequency interference patterns (demonstrable via Fourier transform processes as discussed in Secondary Evidence #3). These wave or frequency interference patterns are clearly "more fundamental" than the material objects that they represent and must emanate from a different, more fundamental level than our material plane.

4. There is compelling evidence to suggest that consciousness does not arise from the physical matter of the brain or any other matter on this physical plane (see Primary Evidence #3), and hence consciousness itself must emanate from a more fundamental (deeper, higher frequency, enfolded) level than this material plane.

5. The work of Alain Aspect and colleagues in 1982 and subsequent related experiments (see Secondary Evidence #1 and #4) that established that photons (light particles) are able to communicate instantaneously, whether they are a few feet or a few billion miles apart, also showed that such communication occurs with no exchange of energy (Aspect 1982, Bouwmeester 1997, Zbinden 2001). Such findings provided novel, reproducible, convincing evidence from many laboratories of a form of communication or signaling occurring without the use of power (unlike radio, TV or cell phone signaling, for example). Such communication between photons (light particles) was also documented to be occurring at speeds far exceeding the

speed with which light can travel on this material plane. It is clear that such signaling must be occurring from a different level which is more fundamental than energy as we perceive it on this physical plane.

6. Other evidence for higher levels of existence can be found in the thousands of researched accounts of Near-Death Experiences (NDEs) that include features highly suggestive of a finer, more energy-dense (higher frequency/lower wavelength) realm or realms, including nonlocality and extraordinary awareness of interconnectedness; instantaneous telepathic exchanges of information in a timeless, placeless dimension; extraordinarily enhanced light, colors and radiance of everything including beings; and, in some cases, a variety of other "unearthly" environmental features. In addition, phenomena such as congenitally blind individuals having the capability of seeing are highly suggestive of function at a different level than our physical plane (see Primary Evidence #1).

7. Our "world" that we see as mountains, oceans, buildings, planets, etc., is illusionary at its core yet real in its perception. This is the basis for mystics speaking of the illusionary nature of our world. Both this plane and its deeper counterparts can *all* be thought of as "real" or forms of "reality"—this may be the easiest way to think of them. Alternatively, all (or all but the deepest level of pure consciousness) could be thought of as illusionary depending upon one's vantage point and orientation.

8. In addition to physicists such as Bohm and philosophers such as Plato and Spinoza postulating deeper, more fundamental levels of reality underlying (or within) this physical plane, numerous spiritual and mystical traditions have espoused this general concept for centuries. There exists a sizeable literature (which has grown exponentially in recent decades) delineating a huge variety of "transcendent" or "mystical" experiences related to numerous spiritual and mystical

traditions along with their various associated techniques for accessing "higher dimensions." While these experiences are generally very individualized, there are a number of features that are commonly encountered which suggest that the experiences involve a deeper level (or levels) beyond this physical plane, including telepathic, instantaneous communication; various types of Peak Experiences and uncommon instantaneous insights (see Secondary Evidence #5); enhanced environmental fluidity and thought responsiveness; and timeless, placeless experiences with nonlocal features transcending this dimension. Some of these experiences include a frank awareness of being out of one's body (so-called Out-of-Body Experiences or OOBEs). In recent years, individuals such as Robert Monroe and numerous others who have pioneered and delineated a variety of techniques for transcending one's body have developed specific methodologies to scientifically study the techniques and their results and, in some cases, have made attempts to characterize and to chart other dimensions. Given that our conventional or mainstream approaches to science have largely equated with materialism, much of the study of these techniques has been beyond the realm of traditional science as we have come to know it. Nevertheless, a growing percentage of our population is becoming aware that everyone has the capability to transcend one's body and brain (e.g., via NDEs and other OOBEs), and once one has had such experiences, it is no longer a question of whether or not such phenomena occur but rather how and why they occur and how the experiences can be helpful.

B. THEORY *of* REALITY SECONDARY EVIDENCE

7. Evidence for Particle and Wave Aspects of Subatomic Structures (as Documented by Physicists) and for How These Components Parallel the Particle and Wave Aspects of Consciousness, Energy and Matter

1. The extensive field of quantum mechanics (which is a branch of physics) is primarily concerned with characterizing the dual particle-like and wave-like behavior and interactions of matter and energy, particularly at the subatomic (smaller than atoms) level. The evidence that both matter and energy have particle and wave aspects (which coexist within each of them) and that matter and energy can be converted back and forth is overwhelming and is now accepted by essentially all of mainstream physics. These concepts—along with the ideas that (1) subatomic particles such as electrons are not precise entities but rather "ensembles" of potentials or possibilities without specific locations or dimensions *until we observe them* and (2) the way the observer interacts with the ensemble (e.g., the type of experiment one does to interact with it) determines which aspect (particle or wave) is detectable and which aspect remains hidden—became necessary as the 20th century unfolded in order to explain a wide range of experimental observations which

could not be accounted for by classical Newtonian physics (Einstein 1935, 1936; Heisenberg 1971).

2. One way to clearly demonstrate the dual particle and wave aspects of an electron, for instance, is to fire an electron directly at a detector screen that will produce a tiny point of light where the electron strikes the screen, thus revealing a specific location and the electron's PARTICLE aspect. On the other hand, the WAVE manifestation of the electron allows it to simultaneously behave in ways that no particle can. If an electron is fired at a barrier with two narrow slits cut into it, the electron is able to pass through BOTH slits at the same time due to its WAVE aspect. The dual particle and wave aspects of light were first demonstrated by the famous double-slit experiment in 1801 by Thomas Young utilizing sunlight as a light source (**figure 6**). Further experimental evidence has shown that all matter (and energy) possesses both particle and wave characteristics and that any particle (including electrons, photons, atoms and molecules) will act as a particle when one does

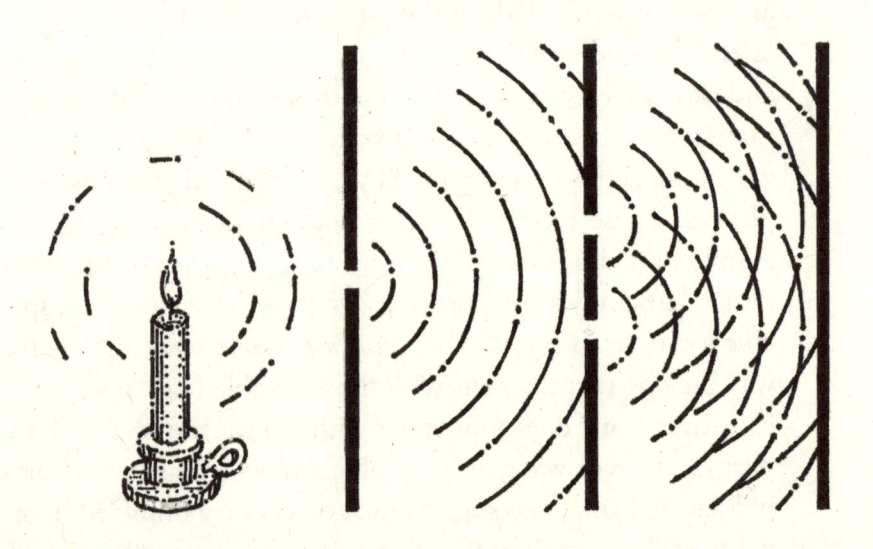

Figure 6. Adaptation of Young's Double-Slit Experiment

an experiment to measure its particle-like features and will act as a wave when one does an experiment designed to measure its wave-like properties.

3. It is important to note that the wave aspects of any of these particles cannot be observed directly using our senses, our brains or any of the materialistic sensing devices we have developed on this plane. In other words, electrons, photons, atoms and molecules behave as waves (with indefinite location) until we observe them. This is completely consistent with our brain cells responding to Fourier transform wave functions (see Secondary Evidence #3) of a plaid cloth, for example, and converting them into the material (particle) aspects of a plaid cloth so that we can see and experience it as "matter" in this physical world as we know it. Again, the brain is acting as a receiver and transducer of a wide range of deeper, finer, waveform, consciousness-based information to be converted to sights, sounds, material textures, etc., to be understood and experienced as "material" (particle aspect) on this material plane. The brain also acts as a receiver of material (particle aspect) information from the body and our senses, which it transcribes into the deeper, finer, waveform, "informational-at-all-levels" language of consciousness and transmits to our deeper, nonlocal (see below and Secondary Evidence #4) conscious selves for comprehension, use and memory storage.

4. It is also important to contemplate the observation that in their wave manifestations, electrons, photons, atoms and molecules no longer possess traits of objects, and they do not even possess any location or dimensions. These characteristics reflect that this deeper wave manifestation of these particles is BEYOND TIME AND SPACE as we know it here on this material plane, and this in turn is a reflection that time and space, as Einstein envisioned, are NOT absolute in their nature—rather they are material manifestations of this plane of existence and of the

various transducers (including our brains) that help us to function here.

5. In recent years, physicists and astronomers have verified that the same type of particle and wave aspects (and the resulting wave interference patterns and effects) apply to photons of light originating from distant stars billions of light years from earth even though such photons originated billions of years ago and are just being observed now on earth. It is useful to deeply consider that the information recorded in these light waves has been registered and retained unchanged for billions of years. When this wave information hits the retinae of our eyes and is processed and transcribed by our visual systems and brains, we can utilize the information in its material form and experience the light of the star as part of this material (particle aspect) universe.

6. The work of Alain Aspect and colleagues in the early 1980s provided proof of the "entanglement" of particles and that they can instantaneously affect one another (see Secondary Evidence #1). This concept (which has subsequently been verified in numerous other laboratories and is now broadly accepted within physics) in turn provides evidence for the phenomenon of *nonlocal space*, which is an underlying multidimensional space that does not include matter (nor time or distance) but rather is composed of probability waves and possibilities—akin to the wave aspects discussed above. Within this nonlocal space, location does not exist as we know it on this material plane and that is why everything can instantaneously (much faster than the speed of light or any material object) communicate with everything else regardless (independent) of distance and time. By its nature, this nonlocal space is generally hidden from our materially oriented senses and brains, yet there are components of it which complement and constantly influence everything in our physical universe. The invisible wave function influ-

ences, complements and is intrinsically linked to the visible particle function. Analogously, our physical bodies and brains are influenced, complemented and intrinsically linked to our consciousness.

7. In recent years, it is becoming increasingly clear to scientists that quantum physics and quantum mechanics have important applications to biological systems because of the recognition that it is simply not possible to explain or account for the behavior of living organisms by somehow adding up the behaviors of all of an organism's isolated components (see Secondary Evidence #1 and #2). In other words, the whole is clearly equal to more than the sum of its parts—and rather than perceiving a living organism as a collection of separate objects or components, it is important to recognize the overwhelming coherence (see Secondary Evidence #2) in all living systems down to the cellular and subcellular (smaller than cells) levels. Nobel laureate and physical chemist Ilya Prigogine (Prigogine 1984) documented in great detail the self-organizing capabilities of living matter, including the incorporation of unstructured chaotic matter into a structure of dynamic ordered coherence (see also Secondary Evidence #1 and #2), and physicists such as Herbert Fröhlich (Fröhlich 1968) and Giuseppe Vitiello (Vitiello 2001) have extended such observations by revealing that within living organisms, various characteristics such as the vibrational frequencies of cells and molecules come into phase (or sync) with each other to form a coherent system in which the many parts not only *behave* as a whole but actually *become* a whole. In analogous systems (known in physics as Bose-Einstein condensates), the various component parts lose their individual identity and merge into a coherent whole in much the same way that one's liver, lungs or cardiovascular system merge with and constantly and instantaneously share information with the rest of one's body (see Secondary Evidence #2).

8. Consciousness is the fundamental wave aspect in deeper dimensions, including all of what has been labeled as nonlocal space by physicists (and all of what has been referred to as one's "subconscious" by psychologists and psychiatrists). Consciousness manifests as the various attributes and dimensions of the physical world. The particle aspect of one's individual consciousness corresponds to the materially oriented (of this physical dimension) manifestations of one's "inner world" which occur in association with one's day-to-day thoughts, words, actions and other brain-mediated activities as they relate to this physical plane and to time and space (which are of this physical plane).

9. The physical/particle "effects" of consciousness can be measured by materialistic measuring techniques such as electroencephalography (EEG), magnetic resonance imaging (MRI) and positron emission tomography (PET). However, as with other wave aspects of matter and energy in nonlocal space, consciousness cannot be experienced with our senses or measured directly by utilizing our brains or other materialistic measuring techniques.

10. There is a "whole organism" or personal consciousness wave function, as well as wave functions corresponding to every component material part of that organism, including and down to the system, organ, tissue, cellular, molecular, atomic and subatomic levels. In an intact, coherent whole organism, the properties of each part at each level become in sync and merge such that the "consciousness" of the parts is largely subsumed into the identity of the whole. This occurs in the context of constant, ongoing, instantaneous information sharing and interaction among all of the components at all levels (see Secondary Evidence #2).

11. The C Field is an even deeper wave function or " base waveform building block" of all that exists, including all of the wave functions mentioned above which correspond to all matter and to all the material manifestations of our personal consciousness, for example. The C Field is therefore intrinsically (and more deeply) connected to all the other wave and particle functions that have been discussed above (see Secondary Evidence #4).

B. THEORY *of* REALITY SECONDARY EVIDENCE

8. Evidence That "Empty Space" Is Not at All Empty and That It Instead Contains an Incredibly Vast Amount of Energy and Provides Insight into What Is Hidden from Our Materialistic Senses and a Materialistic Conceptualization of the Universe

1. Late in his career, while discussing the concept of space in relation to his special theory of relativity, Einstein proclaimed, "There is no such thing as empty space, i.e., space without field" (Einstein 1995).

2. Prior to that, Max Planck, widely regarded as the founder of quantum physics, had also concluded that the emptiness of space was a myth and provided experimental evidence that space was instead flooded with signals and fields (Planck 1993).

3. The vast amount of "vacant" space cannot, of course, be vacant. Even on our material level of reality, we can see that waves of energy transmitting everything from cell phone signals, to the sun's heat, to a super massive black hole 250 million light years from earth, must travel through "empty space." Something must exist to convey these energies from point A to point B.

4. Take a closer look at a piece of solid bone. As we magnify it, there are ordered bone crystals, spicules and various types of molecular webs. As one continues to magnify, we see atoms which at first appear to be shadowy balls vibrating about fixed points in the molecules. As we magnify more we see less and less, and we seem to be looking at a vacuum. Further magnification reveals something tiny moving about—the nucleus of a hydrogen atom, about 100,000 times smaller than the atom itself. As we magnify further and get to electrons or other smaller subatomic particles, they no longer have a particular location that can be fixed. But where did the bone go? It is clear that what underlies our seemingly solid reality is a vast empty space filled with oscillating fields.

5. If we view space as a dead empty void, then what would this say about ourselves in view of the fact that our bodies and brains are more than 99.9999999999999% "empty"? Are we merely fragile atomic and molecular lattices suspended in the void? Clearly, a great deal more than a "dead void" exists in this percentage of "empty space" which constitutes nearly all of what appears on the surface to be our "solid" physical bodies and brains.

6. Space, which has long been referred to by many as a "quantum vacuum," has more recently become recognized by most physicists as something very different from a vacuum—namely a medium with an energy density exceeding by many orders of magnitude the energy density constituting matter.

7. Utilizing a wide variety of approaches over many years, numerous physicists have come to the conclusion that the amount of energy residing in one cubic centimeter (about the size of a bouillon cube) of "empty space" is greater than the amount of energy contained within all the matter in the known universe. This "known" universe refers, of course, to the material universe on this plane of existence.

8. Dutch physicist M.J. Sparnaay was the first to discover what has been referred to as "zero-point (electromagnetic) energy," or ZPE (Sparnaay 1958). For the electromagnetic field in "empty space," every wave has what is referred to as a "zero point energy," which is the lowest amount of energy that it can have. Sparnaay showed that not only did this energy exist in a vacuum but that it continued to exist at the temperature of absolute zero (-273.15 degrees C or -459.67 degrees F)—a point where all classical forms of energy vanish. The basis for this energy was first predicted by another Dutch physicist, Hendrik Casimir, who showed the existence of a force between two uncharged parallel plates in a vacuum arising from electromagnetic radiation surrounding the plates (Casimir 1948). This force has come to be referred to as the "Casimir effect." If one computes the amount of energy that would be in empty space using the shortest possible wavelength (as determined in accordance with Einstein's general theory of relativity), one finds that a cubic centimeter of space does indeed contain more energy than all of the known "physical" matter in the universe.

9. Subsequently in the 1960s, Nobel laureate Richard Feynman (Feynman 1962) along with John Wheeler, one of Einstein's protégés, produced calculations showing that there is more than enough energy in the volume of a coffee cup to evaporate all of the earth's oceans. Wheeler published a book entitled *Geometrodynamics* (Wheeler 1962) within which he delineated in detail his methods for applying the principles of Einstein's general theory of relativity as he examined the amount of energy involved in quantum fluctuations involving waves at lengths as short as a "Planck length," roughly equal to 1.6 times 10 to the minus 33rd power (or 1.6 divided by 10 with 33 zeros behind it) centimeters. Wheeler showed that when one adds up the total amount of energy involved in the work from the fluctuations mentioned above, the result was 10 to the 94th power (1

with 94 zeros behind it) *grams* per cubic centimeter. A gram, of course, is a unit of *mass* and, utilizing the equation $E=mc^2$, (in which "E" stands for energy, "m" stands for mass and "c" represents the speed of light), one arrives at an *energy* level of 10 to the 104th power of *ergs* (a unit of energy and mechanical work) per cubic centimeter. Such a number FAR outweighs all the energy contained within all of the physical matter in the known universe (by a factor of around 10 to the 24th power, or 1,000,000,000,000,000,000,000, 000 times).

Note: For comparison purposes, as mentioned above, the density of ZPE is around 10 to the 94th power grams per cubic centimeter (gm/cm^3). The density of a human body is around 3 gm/cm^3, and the density of lead is around 11 gm/cm^3).

10. More recently, Steve Lamoreaux, an atomic physicist working at the University of Washington, provided further confirmation of the theoretical concepts of the Casimir force and the prior measurements of Sparnaay, with experimental measurements corroborating values predicted by Casimir's original theories to within an error margin of 5% (Lamoreaux 1997). Overall, there are now over 30 published experimental measurements of the Casimir effect and over 1,000 theoretical papers citing Casimir's work in the physics literature.

11. Modern physics demonstrates that the "empty space" between stars and the space between the particles that make up what we perceive as matter are awash with vast amounts of fluctuating energy. This is not a new revelation, but rather represents knowledge that is many decades old and well proven via replicated experimental evidence.

12. Nevertheless, some physicists continue to argue that the nearly infinite amount of energy contained within such a small area of space must be some kind of mistake. Furthermore, this huge energy factor is generally ignored in various physics calculations

under the rubric of "renormalization" in order that the very large number (which would otherwise be utilized as a cosmological constant) not cause "difficulties" in the interpretation of various cosmic equations and calculations. In this way, scientists and the rest of humanity have largely been able to ignore what might otherwise interfere with a purely materialistic approach to science and to broader reality. In the process, it is clear that the purely materialistic approach ignores all but an infinitesimally small part of what constitutes all that exists.

13. In recent years there has been considerable controversy over whether or not we will be able to tap into the enormous potential energy resource contained within this zero-point energy (ZPE) largely because its extremely high energy densities exist at very high frequencies (corresponding to very low wavelengths) and because our current approaches for effectively and efficiently extracting or converting energy can generally do so only at lower frequencies where the ZPE has relatively low energy densities. Some have speculated that discovering the secret of ZPE and its conversion into useful energy could be the key to opening the door to a unified theory of the universe and to ushering in a "Second Coming" of science. Such speculation is well founded and reflects a deeper understanding that we are missing major components in science and in our perception of reality.

14. From the above, it is clear that despite our attachment to our material universe and our perception that it is generally solid and of lasting substance, what we think of as our physical universe is an almost incomprehensibly miniscule part of all that exists. Within the very structure of space itself and all matter as we know it (which, as mentioned above in reference to our bodies and brains, is more than 99.999999999% space) lies an indwelling reservoir of almost unimaginable energy which

pervades everything that exists. All of this provides us with profound insight into the amount of the universe that is "hidden" or "not showing" to our materialistic human senses and to a purely materialistic way of approaching science and reality.

ANATOMY *of a* SPIRITUAL ADVENTURE

All of us are empowered to embark upon the wildest, most fascinating and most fulfilling spiritual adventures that we can imagine.

A spiritual adventure can generally be visualized utilizing a cyclical display consisting of eight fundamental components, each leading to and/or fueling the next, including *Understanding, Centering, Equipping, Charting, Navigating, Discovering, Sharing,* and *Assisting Others*—which in turn leads to further *Understanding* and a new cycle (see **figure 7**).

Looking inward (with or without the assistance of numerous existing tools and techniques which are delineated in the next section of this book) rather than outward for the answers to one's most profound questions is critical.

Actively charting and navigating one's journey and one's various spiritual adventures gives rise to "knowing" or "experiencing" vs. passively "believing" spiritual fundamentals and various creative results. Such an approach facilitates the unfolding of higher understanding, uncommon creativity and vision, and greater overall effectiveness, all of which are generally accompanied by greater happiness and fulfillment.

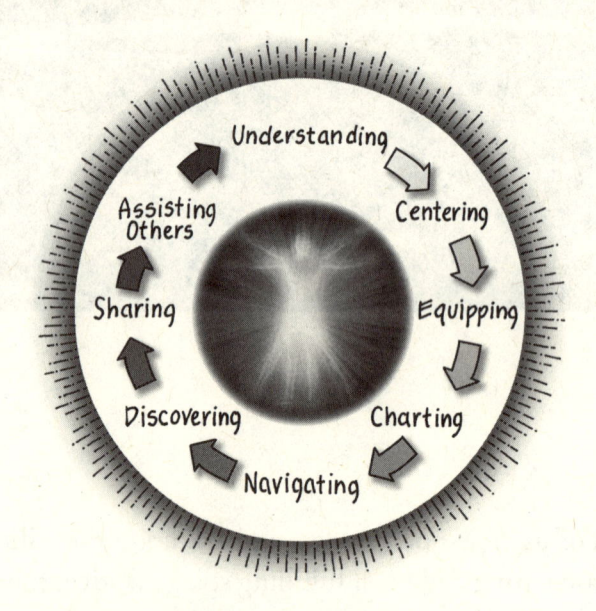

Figure 7. Anatomy of a Spiritual Adventure

In order to help optimize one's spiritual adventures, it is first useful to further define and characterize the eight components graphically depicted above. It will also be useful to provide further details about the tools and techniques that may be of assistance in the course of one's journey and various adventures.

UNDERSTANDING

Understanding is profoundly fundamental to our interacting with and relating to all that exists, including other human and non-human beings and everything else in the universe. In general, our higher forms of human motivation and thought, including love, compassion, and forgiveness, relate to enhanced understanding, and our lower forms of motivation and thought, including fear, anger, aggressiveness and hostility, relate to our lack of understanding of ourselves and others.

Our inability to deeply comprehend the oneness of all that exists and our tendency to fragment our world and to see ourselves as separate from the universe, the earth and other human and nonhuman beings is at the root of our neither being at peace as a species nor as a society.

Higher or enhanced understanding is key to one's balance and one's evolution. It facilitates new spiritual adventures that might otherwise be inaccessible. It is the starting point that allows one to advance spiritually. Whatever higher/enhanced understanding one gains from any insight or integration of concepts regarding one's self and/or how one fits into the universe can fuel new adventures and facilitate greater coherence, discovery and various types of Peak Experiences.

CENTERING

With new and higher understanding, one tends to focus and center oneself around the meaning of the higher understanding and where it might lead on a variety of levels. This, in turn, creates "focused awareness" or enhanced coherence, which sets the stage for increased access to hierarchical levels of information enfolded within the structure of the C Field that would not otherwise be attainable.

The principle involves going from typical random incoherent thought to coherent consciousness and can be as powerful as going from incandescent (incoherent) light to a laser beam in the creation of a hologram. This is particularly relevant given the holographic organization of the universe, the C Field (universal consciousness/information/intelligence), ourselves, our brains and our memory functions.

In addition to new and higher understanding, centering is very much facilitated by deep levels of relaxation and by silencing the ongoing inner chatter that is typically going on during our waking hours on this material plane.

EQUIPPING

Focused awareness, deep relaxation and a still inner voice all lend themselves to the utilization of one or more tools and techniques designed to facilitate Peak Experiences or to otherwise greatly enhance one's creative, intellectual, visionary and/or integrative capabilities.

These tools and techniques range from esoteric metaphysical techniques to relatively simple ways to enhance one's coherence, resilience and equanimity. Although the use of these tools and techniques is by no means required of anyone (some individuals will develop their own tools and techniques intuitively and/or spontaneously, and others will advance without using any named techniques), many will find it very helpful and fascinating to consider and read about the various tools and techniques and how they have worked for others.

After learning about the various tools and techniques, one can engage in a process of "informed choice." In general, one either resonates or doesn't with a given tool or technique at any given time, and this resonance determines what seems "right" or like a "good fit" for the individual. Much of this occurs automatically and without the need for a great deal of analysis—it is beyond the usual process of trying to weigh the pros and cons of a material product or service. In this case, one's deeper subconscious is generally far better at knowing what type of equipping will be the best fit for oneself and one's current needs to advance and evolve.

CHARTING

Once one has developed the ability to center and has assessed the various tools and techniques, it becomes important and relevant to consider and to give intentionality to how one wants to evolve and to what type of underlying motivation one wishes to bring into the experience.

For example, one may wish to enhance one's creativity, vision, understanding or effectiveness in a certain area or may wish to address a very specific question or issue that may be pivotal to oneself at a particular moment. The possibilities here are infinite, and their nature and value come down to a very personal level, which is as it should be.

One's underlying motivation is always important to consider—it is generally more important than what one actually materially does. When one intentionally chooses to bring higher-level motivations into the experience (e.g., love, compassion, selflessness, forgiveness, acceptance, gratitude), as opposed to lower-level motivations (fear, guilt, greed, revenge, selfishness, jealousy), one becomes more coherent and open to other layers of higher-level consciousness/information/intelligence that would otherwise be inaccessible.

NAVIGATING

After one has charted a course and found a tool and/or technique that resonates, it may be useful to read and consider more about the specific tool and technique and various pointers for how to best get results and find one's way, as well as potential pitfalls and elements that may hold one back so that one can get the most out of the experience. If something arises that feels wrong or doesn't seem like the right fit, then it is generally relevant to go back and reconsider other tools and techniques before going further.

When the tool and technique feel right, it can be an incredibly fun, compelling and exhilarating experience to forge ahead and begin experimenting and gaining experience with the tool and/or technique.

The speed with which one obtains results varies considerably with the individual, with the tool and technique, and with the individual's personal circumstances and intentions. Generally, however, it is wise to err on the side of being patient, being grateful and being highly perceptive and open to subtle elements that one might otherwise miss.

DISCOVERING

This is the part of the process that is perhaps the most beautiful and magical in its nature. Einstein observed; "The intellect has little to do on the road to discovery. There comes a leap in consciousness, call it intuition or what you will and the solution comes to you and you don't know how or why." He is not alone. Countless scientists, artists and individuals from virtually every walk of life have echoed the same basic refrain with different words. This is the subtle yet profound nature of discovery and the type of trajectory that allows one to go beyond ordinary day-to-day thought and arrive at uncommon creativity, vision, effectiveness and understanding.

Discovery in this context covers a wide range of phenomena encompassing minor insights to profound and life-changing Peak Experiences and everything in between.

It is time for more of humanity and science to clearly recognize and give intentionality to this process. Everyone has the potential to make use of it, and the results can constitute some of the most wondrous and beautiful experiences in an individual's lifetime, as well as some of the most profound and helpful revelations that any of us can contribute.

A variety of individual nuances will inevitably arise in these processes, and it is useful and important to pay attention to what specifically facilitates and enhances the processes on an individual level. Keeping a journal has been helpful to many in this regard. It is also critical to listen carefully to one's inner voice and intuition as one proceeds along the path to discovery and beyond.

SHARING

Sharing with others and giving without measure are natural outgrowths of the previous components of the spiritual adventure, and they combine to constitute a powerful elixir for the evolution of individuals and humanity.

It is important that one's motivation for sharing be for the benefit (but not the control) of others and that one's intent is to provide others with knowledge and/or tools to empower those individuals and allow them to use their capabilities to find their own way (which will not necessarily match one's original way) as opposed to creating dependence and subservience.

This form of sharing can be very inspirational and helpful to others and deeply fulfilling to the giver. Those who would benefit from whatever message is shared in this way will resonate with whatever component of the message that will be useful for their spiritual adventures and overall journey.

ASSISTING OTHERS

Actively helping, assisting and teaching others under the rubric of giving of oneself for the benefit of others (with no personal agenda or other strings attached) teaches the teacher in unique ways that allow the teacher to experience new understanding and enhanced meaning.

This is a deeply fulfilling aspect of any spiritual adventure, one that gives in return many times over in ways that are unending. It becomes easy to envision how one's new understanding leads to further adventures that build upon a solid and high level foundation when they are based in higher-level motivations.

It also becomes apparent that one's underlying motivation is of critical importance and can make the difference between a very high-level, deeply fulfilling, rewarding and mutually empowering experience on one end of the spectrum and an experience that falls on some other part of the spectrum for both the giver and receiver.

TOOLS *and* TECHNIQUES

1. Peak Experiences (PEs)

Peak Experiences (PEs) generally involve seconds to minutes in which one feels the highest levels of peace, connectedness, happiness, harmony and possibility (Maslow 1994, Wilson 2009). They often are pivotal moments in a person's life and are commonly associated with key insights, "waves of understanding," uncommon creativity and/or "thought balls" (large packages of thoughts/ideas that arrive instantaneously and unfold in real time as they are processed and expressed through our brains).

A variety of tools and techniques have been associated with producing or facilitating PEs or with otherwise deeply enhancing one's creative, intellectual, visionary or integrative understanding and/or capabilities.

What follows is a listing of several of these tools and techniques. It is not meant to be exhaustive but rather to provide some examples of methods that may be useful to anyone seeking to expand their awareness and evolve their understanding and capabilities along their own chosen path.

As one learns about each of these various tools and techniques, it is important to be aware of and "listen" to one's subconscious deeper self, which will generally resonate fairly automatically and instantaneously with tools and techniques that may be the best fit. It is equally important that if any of the tools and/or techniques do not feel right or do not seem like a good fit, then one is wise to heed this feeling and move on to something that does deeply resonate and feel right rather than force any specific tool or technique.

- Near-Death Experiences (NDEs)
- Out-of-Body Experiences (OOBEs)
- Connecting with One's Higher Self (CWOHS)
- After-Death Contact (ADC)
- Past-Life Recall/Regression (PLR)
- Other Tools and Techniques—Meditation, Yoga, Lucid Dreams/Dream Control, Visualization, Hypnosis, Contemplation/Prayer, Triggers/Facilitators
- Enhancing Coherence, Resilience and Equanimity

TOOLS *and* TECHNIQUES

2. Near-Death Experiences (NDEs)

Near-Death Experiences (NDEs) can be extraordinary tools for facilitating PEs and various other capabilities, but given that they generally occur in association with a life-threatening event, they are not planned events or exercises that the individual consciously chooses in advance (Moody 1976, 2010; Sabom 1982; Greyson 1983, 1987, 1998; Ring 1984, 1998, 2008; Morse 1990, 1992; Holdon 2009; Lommel 2010, Carter 2010 and Long 2010).

NDEs are profound events with characteristics that are remarkably consistent from person to person regardless of an individual's age, gender, nationality, ethnicity, marital status, social class, religion, spiritual beliefs, church attendance, etc. (There are some symbolic cultural, religious and age-related nuances and differences in description, but the meaning remains essentially unchanged).

Numerous NDE investigators (e.g., Raymond Moody, Kenneth Ring, Bruce Greyson, Michael Sabom, Pim van Lommel) have described and categorized a variety of features commonly associated with NDEs. These features (which occur in the context of increasingly impaired or absent brain function) include:

1. Feelings of indescribable peace, calm, bliss, comfort and freedom from pain
2. The perception that one is dead or dying
3. Accurate out-of-body views of their own bodies and surrounding environment (e.g., often from a position outside and above their bodies, individuals witness their resuscitation or surgical operation)
4. Moving through a dark space or tunnel toward a distant light
5. Experiencing an otherworldly environment with unbelievably beautiful characteristics, including gorgeous landscapes with dazzling colors and ethereal music
6. Meeting and (telepathically) communicating with deceased relatives and friends
7. Perceiving an unearthly brilliant light or being of light associated with feelings of unconditional love and acceptance and access to unlimited knowledge and wisdom
8. Experiencing a panoramic, detailed, comprehensive, organized, enlightening life review which happens instantaneously and includes every moment in an individual's life, both from the perspective of the individual and from the perspective of others who were affected by the individual
9. Previewing a part of life that is yet to come
10. Perceiving a border, beyond which it will not be possible to return to one's body, and consciously deciding (with or without encouragement) to return to one's earthly body

Science and scientists (including some neuroscientists) have expended an enormous amount of energy and effort trying to relegate the NDE to the arena of invalid illusions, hoaxes or other aberrations and have created a long list of possible alternative explanations (largely rooted in a purely materialistic perspective) for NDEs. Upon detailed analysis, however, none of these explanations is credible (see TOR Primary Evidence #1 for an in-depth discussion), and it is perplexing that more establishment scientists have not been able to look beyond the resistance to accepting these phenomena, particularly in view of the very weak alternative explanations that have been advanced. In reality, the NDE and other related phenomena offer science and scientists (including neuroscientists) vital insights to allow us to evolve beyond a purely materialistic approach to science, life and existence.

NDE TECHNIQUES

As referenced above, there are no specific exercises or techniques that one would suggest to try to induce an NDE. However, there are a number of observations related to numerous NDEs which may be of benefit to all of us as we take some time to reflect and chart our course ahead. These observations include:

1. NDEs commonly involve enhanced mental acuity, including experiencing, thinking about, remembering and reporting independently verifiable details and events from near (e.g., the operating room) and far away (e.g., somewhere else in the hospital or elsewhere on the planet), with many instances of detailed corroboration of events not accessible to one's biological sense organs while one was apparently out of one's body. Such phenomena have been documented to have occurred in the context of *no demonstrable brain function* and flat EEGs leaving

little doubt that the brain is not required for us to continue to exist and function beyond the death of our physical bodies and brains (see also TOR Primary Evidence #1–3).

2. Blind people (including those who have been blind from birth and who have never been able to see while awake or in dreams, and who consequently do not have functioning material brain/eye visual systems) can see during NDEs and OOBEs (Out-of-Body Experiences), and have reported independently verifiable details requiring vision during NDEs (which, as above, has been documented with no demonstrable brain function) and OOBEs. These observations provide further evidence for our existence beyond material brains and bodies. Conventional materialistic science has no way to account for any of these observations (or those in point 1 above).

3. The two most important aspects in self-judgment at death are compassion/love (for others) and knowledge.

4. Much of what we are generally conditioned to feel self-conscious or guilty about in our day-to-day lives is insignificant and self-defeating from a spiritual perspective.

5. Guilt and fear are not high-level motivators; love and compassion are high-level motivators.

6. One's underlying motivation for what one is doing is the most important element of any life activity (even more important than the activity itself) as revealed in the life review process of NDEs.

7. In the life review process (as referenced above in the NDE features), there is no fear (unless brought and/or expected by the individual), no external judgment, coercion, authoritarianism or attempted condemnation. Rather, one faces everything in an unbiased way without the usual psychological defense mechanisms that all of us have "constructed" in this lifetime

with the idea of helping us to "survive." The main reason for the review is to help individuals help themselves to reflect upon what form and circumstance, if any, that they'd like to return in to evolve themselves and others.

WHAT TO EXPECT (NDEs)

One of the greatest values of experiencing an NDE is that one subsequently KNOWS as opposed to BELIEVES that one can and ultimately will exist independently from the physical body and brain. This greatly facilitates a deep understanding of the concept that one's brain and body are temporary vehicles rather than part of one's core identity—a concept that is fundamental to virtually any form of what has been referred to as enlightenment.

A number of other changes have also been documented among individuals who have experienced NDEs (Moody 1976; Greyson 1983; Ring 1984, 1998; Morse 1992; Holdon 2009; Lommel 2010, Carter 2010 and Long 2010). These changes (which generally last for the rest of one's life) include:

1. Decreased or absent fear of death or dying
2. Increased compassion and tolerance for others
3. Increased thirst for knowledge
4. Enhanced appreciation for life
5. Greater interest in spirituality (and less interest in specific religious affiliation)
6. Greater sense of social justice
7. Enhanced intuitive capabilities (precognition, telepathy, perceptive abilities, intuition)

8. Greater understanding of the purpose of life
9. Heightened sense of self-worth

TOOLS *and* TECHNIQUES

3. Out-of-Body Experiences (OOBEs)

Out-of-Body Experiences (OOBEs) commonly occur as a part of NDEs. They can also occur spontaneously or as a result of numerous techniques that have been developed to induce them. Although many perceive OOBEs as rare and difficult to accomplish, everyone has the capability to experience them, and they can serve as natural, helpful tools in a variety of contexts. They have been associated with Peak Experiences as well as various types of enhanced understanding, effectiveness, creativity, vision and coherence.

Although many mystical, spiritual and religious traditions have referenced OOBEs in their teachings, it is not necessary for anyone to subscribe to any of these specific belief systems or traditions in order to have an OOBE.

In the modern era, Robert Monroe, a Virginia businessman and distinguished writer, creator and producer of hundreds of radio and network TV programs, was an early pioneer in this field, and his first book *Journeys Out of the Body* (Monroe 1971) paved the way for a plethora of further books on the subject, along with numerous scientific studies and a host of different techniques to enable OOBEs (Rogo 1983; Monroe 1985, 1994; Stack 1988; Buhlman 1996; Gustus 2011). Over the 50 years since Monroe's early work, it has become recognized that OOBEs are much more widespread in the general public than previously thought, that they constitute a normal human experience which is generally pleasurable and can be advantageous psychologically and otherwise, and that no particular demographic characteristics or beliefs make a person prone to having them.

OOBE TECHNIQUES

As referenced above, the number of techniques that have been advanced to facilitate OOBEs is considerable. The disadvantage of this is that one may feel it is a daunting task to evaluate so many techniques in order to decide which one is best. The advantage of the large number of techniques is that the OOBE phenomenon and its induction is clearly not a "one size fits all" type of undertaking, and individualization of the techniques is plainly indicated. Moreover, one's choice of one or more techniques will generally be fairly automatic and instantaneous based upon one's deeper resonance with the technique(s) rather than a laborious analysis such as one might do when comparing material products. It is also very common for individuals to create their own nuances and modifications of techniques based upon what feels right for them and what works best for them.

Herein I will list two techniques that have been among the easiest to incorporate. The two greatest inhibitors to achieving the out-of-body state are (1) fear (the greatest inhibitor) and (2) the degree of perceived difficulty associated with inducing OOBEs.

These two factors are the basis for the affirmations that are included in the first technique.

OOBE Technique #1

It is important that you deeply realize that there is no question, none whatsoever, that you are entirely capable of having OOBEs if you wish to do so.

First, you must repeat the following affirmations many, many times before going to sleep:

Affirmation #1: It is easy for me to have OOBEs—I induce OOBEs readily and effortlessly.

Affirmation #2: I create my own reality and I am absolutely safe from all harm. Leaving the body is a natural and safe process.

As you continue to repeat these affirmations, visualize yourself floating upward feet first with increasing speed until you are floating over the city or countryside nearby looking down on all that is below.

Continue to repeat the two affirmations and visualize yourself floating, drifting and accelerating upward at whatever speed is right for you.

Now plan to go to sleep for about 3 or 4 hours and set your alarm clock to wake up an hour or two before sunrise.

It may be helpful to listen to some soothing or inspirational music just before bedtime so that you can have it in mind as you go to sleep.

When you awaken, get out of bed and stay up for a short while (the amount of time will vary by individual so it is good to experiment with staying up for times ranging from a few minutes to an hour or so to find out what amount of time works best for you).

While you are awake, try to maintain a quiet, relaxed, focused state. It may be helpful to listen to some relaxing music or to read an inspirational book during this time. Some have also found it useful to take a small amount of caffeine during this period.

Following this 3 to 60 minute period of quiet, relaxed, focused wakefulness, you can prepare to go back to sleep, but this time with the expectation of having an OOBE.

As you begin to get yourself ready to go back to sleep, it is helpful to give yourself your version of the following suggestions:

1. I am now going to have an OOBE.
2. I am going to leave my body with complete awareness of what is happening.
3. I am going to begin to go to back to sleep, but this time I will bring with me my wakeful awareness wherever I go.
4. I am going to have an OOBE that is safe, effortless, fun and exciting.

As you continue to repeat these suggestions, you may drift off to sleep temporarily and then awaken out of your body. Most often this will be in the same room, and you will be able to move about and view your body or move through walls or other material objects. Alternatively, you may find yourself in another dimension of your own inner reality.

You may also find that you drift off to sleep and then awaken still in your body but in a wakefulness-sleep transitional state (hypnagogia) in which your mind is alert and your body and mind are fully relaxed. There is a special energy about this state that is full of possibilities. It is good for you to mark this state and be able to recognize it and come back to it because this is a state that allows one to very effortlessly lift right out of one's body and proceed with an OOBE.

Many individuals simply focus on the hypnagogic state which can be accessed as described above. Alternatively, by making specific suggestions to yourself while falling asleep, you will deeply relax and let go while gently monitoring yourself as you slowly drift off to sleep (this still works best in the hours before sunrise after you have slept for at least a few hours). Instead of having a brief period in which you drift off to sleep, you suggest to yourself that you will maintain your awareness throughout the process until you have reached the hypnagogic state.

During this time, you must keep your mind focused—on your breathing in and out and/or on a simple phrase to remind you of your intent. Some benefit from visualizing and re-creating with all their senses an activity such as driving a car. If you have an intrusive thought or need to scratch or shift your body, go ahead and observe the thought drifting away or briefly scratch or shift then immediately return to your focus as if nothing happened.

When you reach the hypnagogic state, observe it quietly and proceed to use it in a way that is beneficial. As referenced above, it is easy to lift out of one's body and proceed with an OOBE. Alternatively, it can be used to enter and become active in a lucid dream. The hypnagogic state can also be used to directly enhance creativity, even from a passive observational perspective without OOBEs as has been reported by numerous well-known artists and thought leaders throughout history.

OOBE Technique #2

This technique does not involve going to sleep but nevertheless begins with an exercise to promote deep relaxation. Lie on the floor in a comfortable position and focus your attention on taking slow, deep breaths, pausing at the beginning and end of each breathing cycle. Following this, it is helpful to begin a process of tightening and then relaxing muscles for several seconds each, beginning with one's toes, feet, calves, thighs, buttocks, torso, chest, fingers, hands, forearms, upper arms, shoulders, neck and face muscles. With each muscle group, you should progressively feel the relaxation of that group as well as the whole rest of your body. As you focus on the relaxation of each individual group of muscles, you also become aware of the warmth associated with relaxation which progressively envelops your body as you maintain a deep and relaxing breathing pattern.

After you have attained a state of deep relaxation, focus your awareness on the image of a thick rope hanging from the ceiling of the room to a point just above your chest. Create as clear of an image as you can and feel for the rope with your inner awareness. See that the rope is 3 inches thick and white—and as you reach out to grasp it, feel it in your hand as soft, satiny and very sturdy to easily be able to support your weight. Feel the tension as you pull on the rope and begin to lift yourself off the ground as you grasp the rope with your other hand. Re-create the same inner sensations of pulling yourself up and climbing the rope one hand over the other. As your entire body lifts off the ground, you keep climbing, and the climbing gets more and more effortless until you find yourself above the ceiling of the room and into the clouds, looking down on all that is below. As you continue to move through the clouds, you become lighter and lighter to the point where you no longer need the rope and you subsequently simply float upward and realize that you are out of your body.

An alternative "inner activity" visualization that has also worked well involves focusing awareness on the activity of swinging on a large, sturdy playground swing as most of us used to do as children. Again, it is very helpful to try to re-create with your inner awareness all of the sights and sounds of getting up on a swing and beginning to swing, as well as the feel of all of the various sensations associated with swinging back and forth, going higher and higher. Feel yourself pulling on the chains with your arms, as you kick with your feet and legs to pump higher. Eventually, as you feel the rhythmic motion and gravitational pull back and forth, you get to a point where you get lighter and lighter and you don't need the swing anymore—and at this point you lift or drift out of your body.

Many will find that these focused inner awareness activities lead to a vibrational state in which one feels one's entire body is vibrating. Sometimes this can be extremely coarse and intense, particularly if one does not have prior experience with OOBEs. In this circumstance, continue to relax and "go with the flow" of this as a normal and safe phenomenon (any fear or urgency will immediately put an end to the process and cause one to revert back into one's physical body), and wait for the vibrations to settle down and become very refined. At this point, it will be easy to lift right out of one's body and proceed with an OOBE.

Some individuals have found that doing the above focused inner awareness activities (e.g., climbing a rope or swinging on a swing) just before going to bed allows them to lift out of their bodies as they fall to sleep or to awaken out of their bodies after initially falling to sleep.

Another aspect that applies to both OOBE Techniques #1 and #2 is that many have found it very useful to make a recording of their own voice giving themselves the suggestions as listed above so that they can play back the recording to help induce the OOBE. Hearing one's own voice giving the suggestions is often a powerful component for inducing these experiences.

WHAT TO EXPECT (OOBEs)

As is the case with NDEs, one of the greatest values of OOBEs is KNOWING as opposed to BELIEVING that one can and indeed will exist beyond the body and brain. This, in itself can take much fear out of one's life since many of our fears as a species are ultimately rooted in the fear of death. Decreased or absent fear of death is clearly one of the elements that follows OOBEs associated with NDEs, and although OOBEs unassociated with NDEs have not been studied nearly as extensively, it is very likely that a strong correlation should exist.

Numerous books have been written over the past half century that delineate numerous variations of OOBEs along with more sophisticated molding of these experiences to fit various purposes and motivations. They can serve as a fascinating and exciting vehicle to expand one's awareness and knowledge base about oneself and the universe, to facilitate deeper forms of communication with one's higher self or with other forms of guidance, and/or to enhance one's higher level understanding, creativeness, vision and effectiveness.

Although scientific studies of these phenomena per se have been limited (understandably so since most of these phenomena cannot be measured or accounted for by materialistic science), studies of individuals participating in programs designed to focus consciousness and/or facilitate OOBEs at the Monroe Institute have suggested benefits in the realms of self-efficacy (e.g., greater understanding of life, clearer sense of purpose, enhanced ability to resolve important issues or challenges) and life satisfaction (Danielson 2010).

There are numerous reports of OOBEs (and the OOBE aspect of NDEs) involving individuals experiencing a separate realm or level of existence in which the individual felt that they had access to the sum total of all knowledge in a state beyond time and space where past, present and future seemed to coexist. Numerous others have experienced and reported various durations of teaching and guidance (generally via some form of telepathic communication) which may or may not directly relate to specific questions or conundrums that they sought to resolve as part of their motivation for getting out of their body and brain.

Often, following these episodes, individuals will have new answers to questions or conundrums that they did not have before or new creativity that allows them to make discoveries. Yet even in the most fulminate situations in which individuals have felt an access to all knowledge, this unlimited knowledge base has not stayed with them when they get back into their body and brain. This is consistent with the enhanced coherence and focused awareness required to experience OOBE phenomena and with various focused states of consciousness facilitating connectedness to hierarchical levels of consciousness, information, intelligence and experience within more universal and/or deeper aspects of the C Field.

Experiences such as those referenced above, while generally beyond words and difficult to describe in our usual language, have, in many cases, had a profound and lasting beneficial effect (e.g., enhanced intuitive capabilities, uncommon understanding) on the individual (see Primary Evidence #1). They are also consistent with the need to be (at least somewhat) free of one's brain (and one's materialistic brain processes) in order to access these types of experiences. They also reflect some of the brain's limiting or filtering functions which are commensurate with this physical materialistic plane.

Ultimately, as referenced above in regard to other types of Peak Experiences, the value of these phenomena and experiences comes down to a very individual and personal level as it should. From the time that humans are born on this planet, they are taught to look outward and to look to various institutions for meaning and for answers. In reality, we need to look inward for answers. Everything that is needed is inward. The JOURNEY itself (and active participation as opposed to passive acceptance) is of great importance. As Einstein observed, "The pursuit of knowledge is more valuable than its possession."

TOOLS *and* TECHNIQUES

4. Connecting with One's Higher Self (CWOHS)

There are a number of techniques that involve attempts to be more fully connected with one's higher self, which can also be thought of as one's deeper subconscious self, the part of oneself that is closest to All That Is (alternatively designated as God or the Divine), or the part of All That Is that is within oneself. In any of these contexts, one is "going within" and generally attempting to access one's deeper, inner subconscious self, which is far more capable and far more aware in a universal sense than what we normally think of as our "conscious selves" relative to this material plane.

Several techniques have been published and advocated, including various forms of meditation and yoga, techniques related to OOBEs, intuitive awakening of one's inner guide, visualization techniques, and simply stilling oneself and listening to one's inner self/guide (Gee 1999, Coit 2002).

CWOHS TECHNIQUE

This technique is an amalgamation of the above methods and builds upon the OOBE techniques which are already provided above.

Lie down in a comfortable position where you will not be disturbed. Still your mind.

Make it known through your own intention, either silently or aloud, that you are seeking to connect with your higher self or inner guide and that the presence of this part of your consciousness (and anything involved in producing its presence) will not frighten you.

It is also helpful to give intention to your motivation for this connection, whether it is for general guidance, expansion of your own reality or to help you resolve a specific question or conundrum that is important to you.

Then proceed with either of the two OOBE techniques referenced above and free yourself from your physical body and brain. In the OOB state, everything becomes much more thought-responsive so it becomes relevant and pertinent for you to simply focus your awareness on an affirmation such as "I will now experience my higher self." Give full intentionality to this, including the aspect that it will happen instantaneously and maintain your focus regardless of what happens. It is not uncommon for one to experience loud noises, humming or buzzing sounds, mild to severe vibrations, or other types of rather extreme inner motion including the feeling of being drawn or pulled forcefully into a giant vacuum.

After a while the noises and/or motion phenomena cease, and you may experience what has been referred to as a dimension of indescribable light and unlimited knowledge which clearly represents an expansion of our usual material reality and generally corresponds to some of the higher frequencies that we are missing with a purely materialistic approach to reality (see TOR Secondary Evidence #8). This type of experience is often life-changing and is commonly described as one of the most profound experiences of a person's life.

WHAT TO EXPECT (CWOHS)

There is great variability in how profound these experiences can be—ranging from minor and subtle resolution of specific day-to-day issues or questions, to the type of experience referenced in the above section which is profound, dramatic and life-changing. The more subtle techniques tend to be much easier to induce and have less potential for frightening or alarming the individual who is working with the technique.

Communications can range from vague or subtle intuitions which seem to pull one in a particular direction on an issue or question to very complex conversations with clearly perceivable entities representing one's higher self, one's "inner guide" or some other form of being such as a being of light.

Communication in such experiences is generally with some form of telepathy and ideas are often received in the form of voluminous packages of thought ("thought balls") that need to be rolled out in real time by the brain in order to be fully expressed on this physical plane.

Such experiences often shake the foundation of one's perception of reality and enhance one's intuitive and spiritual capabilities in ways that appear to be similar to individuals who have NDEs. They allow one's understanding of oneself and the universe to evolve in very meaningful and important ways, and they empower one to be far more effective by accessing all kinds of capabilities that would otherwise be latent within oneself.

TOOLS *and* TECHNIQUES

5. *After-Death Contact (ADC)*

The phenomenon of connecting with deceased loved ones, friends, colleagues and others often occurs in association with NDEs as referenced above. Approximately 30–40% of individuals having NDEs have reported recalling such an experience. Communication with these deceased individuals generally takes place through some form of telepathy, and they often appear to be younger and healthier than the individual experiencing the NDE remembers. There are a number of documented cases in which the NDEer meets with someone that they feel very close to but don't recognize and later find out that the deceased person was someone that they were too young to remember in this physical lifetime. In other instances, the NDEer does not even realize that the deceased person they are meeting has died, and they later learn of this after returning to their physical brain and body.

A variety of other techniques for communicating with deceased individuals exist and often have involved individuals who are purported to have specific skills in this regard (and I suspect that many indeed do). Still others have suggested specific techniques that individuals can utilize for themselves. In the early 1990s, Raymond Moody, a psychiatrist who was an early pioneer in the field of NDEs, did a lot of work with ADC and wrote a book with Paul Perry called *Reunions* (Moody 1993) in which he details his work with ADC techniques involving the phenomenon of mirror gazing (gazing into reflective surfaces of various types with focused awareness to open one up to new dimensions).

Individuals experiencing OOBEs unrelated to NDEs have also reported consciously meeting and communicating with deceased loved ones, friends, colleagues and others, and the technique listed below builds upon this phenomenon.

ADC TECHNIQUE

Openly declare to the person before they die, if possible, and/or at the time you are trying to make contact with them that their presence will not frighten you and that they needn't be concerned about this. Invite them into your consciousness. These aspects are important and need to be clearly communicated by you either out loud, internally or (preferably) both.

Before attempting to connect with a departed individual, it is often useful to find and review old pictures or mementos to help re-create their energy and inspire you to be able to connect with them in another dimension.

It is important to be entirely relaxed and unafraid, and to avoid an attitude of intense anticipation which seems to be counterproductive.

Then proceed with OOBE Technique 1 or 2 above (or any other you may choose).

When you find yourself in an OOB state, focus your awareness on the energy of the individual. It is fine to simultaneously picture their face, hear their voice, remember an experience with them in this physical world, etc., but it is even more important that you feel their energy within you. Then again declare your intent to meet with this individual now (instantaneously) and be prepared to "go with the flow" of anything that happens, including loud noises, mild to intense vibrations, other inner motions, various visual phenomena, etc. After any of these various phenomena have played out and ceased or nearly ceased, you may experience ADC. In other instances, no phenomena will intervene, and the communication will be instantaneous.

WHAT TO EXPECT (ADC)

As with other techniques, there is wide variability in the depth of these experiences from person to person and from session to session. The connectedness with deceased individuals can range from subtle feelings of their presence to a very clear vision of the individual engaging in complex, new conversations. As with NDE communications of this sort, the form of communication is generally telepathic in nature.

Meetings of this nature are clearly perceived as real and not dreams, fantasies or some other aberration, and they often have a profound effect on the individual who experiences them, expanding the individual's perception of reality and enhancing their intuitive and spiritual capabilities in ways that appear to be similar to the effects produced by NDEs.

There are many documented cases in which participants in ADC exercises seek to engage a specific deceased individual but end up connecting with someone different who is generally a relative or friend of the individual they had intended to see.

In other cases, the ADC exercises may yield only subtle or vague feelings of the deceased individual at the time the exercises take place, and subsequently the deceased individual will appear to the person in another setting associated with falling asleep, waking up or some moment of focused awareness totally unrelated to sleep.

As with NDEs and other OOBEs, one of the greatest values of these experiences is that one KNOWS as opposed to BELIEVES that one can and ultimately *will* survive after death of the physical brain and body, which makes it clear that the brain and body are temporary vehicles rather than our core identity. Such experiences also often shake the very foundation of one's perception of reality and allow one's understanding of oneself and the universe to evolve in ways that are uncommon and important.

ADC experiences can also be very comforting and fulfilling for both the deceased individuals and those trying to connect with them. All of us have the capability of generating such experiences. Although it has been common for individuals to seek out others to try to connect them with deceased individuals, it seems far preferable for individuals to chart their own course, control their own destiny and to be free of dependency upon others in this regard. In this setting, the experiences become more personal, more meaningful and more likely to involve profound evolution of the individual instigating the experience.

TOOLS *and* TECHNIQUES

6. Past-Life Recall/Regression (PLR)

The phenomenon of reincarnation has been studied by individuals such as Ian Stevenson, professor and chair of psychiatry at the University of Virginia, who has carried out extensive systematic research over more than three decades involving over 3,000 children (generally ages 2–6) from 12 countries with spontaneous, vivid memories of past-life experiences (Stevenson 1974, 1997). These experiences included sites, persons and events that these individuals had not and could not have encountered in their present lifetime, with details such as names of their previous spouse and children, specific elements of their living environment, other friends and neighbors (sometimes far into the past) and even speaking fluently in ancient languages and dialects (with subsequent verification by language scholars) not currently used on this physical plane.

Stevenson and colleagues interviewed not only the child who had the experience and next of kin, but also the family of the "reincarnated" deceased person, which often resulted in extraordinarily detailed agreement between the child's story and the story from the other family sometimes hundreds or thousands of miles away. Reviewing the details of individual cases makes it clear that these children are recalling bona fide details of some other existence on this physical plane which they could not in any way have been physically exposed to in their present lifetime. Some have suggested that this proves reincarnation (some form of which would seem to be the most plausible conclusion, as referenced below), while others have suggested that the observations could also be explained by the idea of so-called nonlocal consciousness, with the brain/consciousness of the present-day child resonating with the consciousness of the deceased individual. IN EITHER CASE, memories and experiences of a prior existence are residing within the consciousness of the individual currently "living" on this physical plane.

Over the years, many psychiatrists and psychologists have utilized PLR techniques, which generally have involved hypnosis of patients (sometimes for other reasons) followed by the patient either spontaneously beginning to talk about past lives or by the psychiatrist or psychologist guiding the patient to specifically attempt to recall past lives. Many of these sessions are designed to explain phobias or other current life problems and to help the patient to understand the origins of these problems and to resolve them.

Many psychiatrists and psychologists have dismissed such regressions as fantasy or repetition of things learned in this lifetime. However, it is exceedingly difficult to attribute Stevenson's carefully documented accounts to such explanations. Moreover, many other psychiatrists—such as Raymond Moody, referenced above in regard to NDEs and ADC—and psychologists have become convinced of the usefulness and veracity of such regressions. In Moody's case, he had been a lifelong doubter of regression hypnosis until he underwent a Past-Life Regression performed by a colleague psychologist in which he vividly recalled nine past lifetimes on this planet. Moody subsequently engaged in a considerable amount of his own research, which further convinced him of the value and validity of past life regression (Moody 1990).

Although the term "reincarnation" is one that is widely utilized, discussed and accepted in many world cultures, what we remember as past lives could more appropriately and more accurately be characterized as prior experiences within an ongoing, eternal and timeless existence. In this sense, our timeless, spaceless essence of pure consciousness takes on or inhabits various temporary vehicles (including various physical brains and bodies) in order to learn and gain experience, but the core essence of our being remains outside the reincarnation process.

These past lives or experiences are forever stored as part of our consciousness, and they can be accessed by our deeper subconscious selves. Our current materially focused existence on this plane and in this lifetime keeps our brains focused on the day-to-day happenings and "noise" associated with all material things which appear to be in the "here and now." The brain is very limited by the amount of information that it can receive and process at any one point in time, and the filtering mechanism associated with the material aspects of our thought processes tends to allow us to recall or focus upon only those aspects of past lives that are relevant to this lifetime or are otherwise triggered by events, locations, people, or other phenomena that remind us of those prior existences (Chadwick 1988).

PLR TECHNIQUE

Besides spontaneous Past-Life Recall and hypnotic Past-Life Regression, a number of other techniques have been suggested to allow individuals to explore their own past lives/experiences. The method presented here represents an amalgamation of various techniques and takes advantage of the OOBE and CWOHS techniques referenced above.

The basic intent of this technique is to project yourself into one or more of your past lives using your higher self as a vehicle or guide for this journey.

In a quiet place where you will not be disturbed, follow the same techniques outlined above to achieve an OOBE and to connect with your higher self.

If you establish a strong connection with your higher self, allow your higher self to take you along to a previous existence and follow that lead to wherever it takes you.

If you are unable to establish a strong connection with your higher self but nevertheless find yourself in an OOB state, take the opportunity to lift yourself far above the earth and then, looking down at all that is below, suggest to yourself that you will gradually descend and come down easily in a place and time that reflects one of your past existences.

In addition to the phenomenon of gradually descending, you may experience other somewhat unusual sensations, sights and/or sounds such as moving through progressively lower densities, vibrations, moving through a tunnel, experiencing various colors of lights or sounds such as buzzing or humming. Any of these unusual sights, sounds or sensations are best taken in stride without alarm—ride them out and stay relaxed. Let your deeper subconscious self do the work and be open to (and move forward with) any impressions that you begin to receive.

If you are confused or somewhat disoriented, it may be helpful to ask focused questions (generally telepathically) about where you are, what year it is, why this event is significant to you, or how you or others might benefit from experiencing this particular episode. These focused questions are particularly helpful if you have made a strong connection with your higher self, but may still be helpful if you are not aware of such a connection.

You can generally choose to either directly experience all of the events that are attached to the scene as it plays out or to alternatively remain above the scene and be somewhat detached from it while watching it play out. Both perspectives have much to offer—the first is more dramatic and stunning, while the second can offer more understanding as to why something happened and how it continues to affect you.

As the scene plays out, it is common for the individual to identify with one person in the scene and to feel some connection to some aspect of their current life. Most of the time, the PLR experiences seem to play out according to themes or specific meanings as opposed to following any sort of timeline.

It is important that if you have fears or concerns about doing any of this, do not push forcefully ahead—wait until it feels right and follow your intuition or higher self to resolve whatever is causing your fears or discomfort before proceeding with any attempts to project yourself into a prior existence.

WHAT TO EXPECT (PLR)

As with prior techniques described in this section, PLR experiences vary considerably from person to person and episode to episode, ranging from vague visions, feelings or general awareness of past existences to very vivid full-spectrum sensory experiences with fulminate accompanying emotional components. Although some individuals are able to have profound and life-changing experiences almost immediately upon trying a given technique, there is a tendency for PLR to become easier over time with added experience and practice.

Sometimes, one may experience relatively nondescript perceptions or feelings during an exercise and later have rather vivid flashes associated with other elements on this physical plane which trigger deeper memories of a prior existence (e.g., various locations, sights, sounds, smells, tastes, human and nonhuman beings, music, works of art, etc.). If, at the time of such a triggering effect, one is engaged in day-to-day activities with active material thoughts going through one's consciousness, then the experiences will generally be only very brief flashes or snippets. One's awareness generally needs to be very focused or coherent in order for a prolonged, uninterrupted experience to play forward.

Gradually, individuals often come to recognize particular undefinable feelings, associated with various triggers, that are suggestive of a prior life and its circumstances. Such indicators, along with more robust experiences as delineated above, collectively enable one to put together many pieces of past existences if one is interested in doing so.

Some past lives accessed in this way have been documented by going to specific locations and/or researching historical documents, and anyone can seek to document their own experiences. These sorts of PLR experiences have not been studied in as much detail as the spontaneous PLR experiences of children.

Numerous psychologists and psychiatrists have reported substantial therapeutic benefits for patients as a result of PLR techniques in clinical practice. Ultimately, however, the value of these and other PLR phenomena is best assessed by the individuals who are seeking to benefit from them. It is common for individuals involved in PLR to report that they have a much deeper understanding of themselves and their current circumstances, and that they have advanced themselves psychologically and spiritually.

As with the ADC techniques referenced above, although many have tended to seek assistance from others to perform PLR through hypnosis or other techniques, it is clearly possible for individuals to induce PLR on their own and, by so doing, to have more control over their experience and more of a role in charting their own path.

TOOLS *and* TECHNIQUES

7. Other Tools and Techniques

The five tools and techniques referenced above are by no means the only ones capable of facilitating Peak Experiences or otherwise deeply enhancing one's creative, intellectual, visionary or integrative capabilities. The tools and techniques listed above do provide some of the clearest examples of phenomena that involve separating one's consciousness from one's body and brain (the accomplishment of which can bring great rewards in and of itself) and also constitute phenomena that can be accomplished without the necessity of building dependencies on anyone or anything outside oneself, unless one is so inclined.

In this section, a variety of other techniques that may also be useful are briefly mentioned. Although an enormous amount of information already exists for the vast majority of these phenomena, some references that may assist in one's further exploration are provided. For many individuals, one or more of the techniques in this section may resonate much more fully with their inclinations and needs than any of the techniques in the prior sections.

MEDITATION

Meditation is a broad term encompassing a great diversity of techniques designed to focus one's awareness to facilitate spiritual realization. Almost any of the tools and techniques in the above sections can be looked upon as involving some form of in-depth meditation. On the other side of the spectrum, meditation techniques can be some of the most subtle and simple methods of all for spiritual advancement. Most spiritual traditions include meditation in some form as part of their teachings and practice (Roche 1998, Freke 2000).

Meditation commonly involves stilling the mind and fixing one's attention on a word or phrase (referred to as a mantra), an object (such as a candle) or a process (such as one's breathing). Many techniques involve an individual being completely still and relaxed, while others (such as T'ai Chi) may involve physical movement.

YOGA

Yoga encompasses several different systems and techniques to promote psycho-physical well-being and spiritual advancement through a greater understanding of one's deeper self and through feelings of connectedness with the rest of the universe. Numerous classifications have been offered by various authors and traditions, but generally the different systems and techniques can be thought of as involving various aspects of breathing, posture and meditation (Hewitt 1990, Freke 2000).

Although yoga was originally associated with Hinduism, its various forms have in more recent times become more broadly accepted as having the potential to supplement any religious practice or to be utilized independently of any religious practice. Although seldom included in various listings of forms of yoga, the concept and principles underlying Surat Shabd Yoga (the yoga of the sacred sound current) have been particularly interesting and inspirational.

LUCID DREAMS/ DREAM CONTROL

These techniques have been advanced particularly as vehicles to improving one's creativity, one's problem solving skills and one's overall personal growth. Substantial evidence for the possibility of remaining awake and aware during one's dreams and for actively participating in, controlling, remembering and subsequently utilizing one's dreams has been presented by Stephen LaBerge, a Stanford University sleep researcher, and others beginning in the 1980s (LaBerge 2009).

VISUALIZATION

Most visualization techniques are forms of meditation that use the power of one's visual imagination to facilitate various states of mind with the goal of enhancing personal creativity, relaxation, performance, understanding, intuition and spiritual awareness. These techniques have broad application across many life arenas and are compatible with virtually any spiritual tradition (Gawain 2002).

HYPNOSIS

Hypnosis has been referenced above in regard to PLR therapeutic techniques as utilized in psychiatry and psychology. Although some form of hypnosis has arguably been used in almost every culture historically, the phenomenon of self-hypnosis and its potential usefulness in general society have only come to light in more recent decades. Several techniques have been suggested and utilized to improve one's general physical and mental well-being and more specifically to improve creativity, learning, self-esteem, relaxation, athletic performance, and to assist with numerous health and lifestyle issues such as weight loss, smoking cessation and overcoming various phobias.

CONTEMPLATION/PRAYER

Contemplation and silent prayer can both be classified as forms of meditation. Contemplation generally involves stilling one's material thoughts, focusing on specific questions or issues, and listening for intuitive answers. Prayer can offer an opportunity for individuals to express gratitude and to share hopes and fears with a Higher Power. Both need to be more than petitioning a Deity with one's personal desires, and neither should be based primarily in fear or guilt in order for them to bring out the highest levels of individual consciousness (Hadley 1996).

TRIGGERS/FACILITATORS

There are numerous triggers or facilitators that make it more likely that an individual will have a Peak Experience or otherwise experience enhanced creativity, understanding, vision or integrative capability. Examples of such triggers include inspirational locations (e.g., mountains, bodies of water, sunrises or sunsets, or other specific locations where one feels creative energy), contact with other specific humans or nonhumans, contact with water, specific music or works of art, etc. These triggers tend to be very individualized, and hence it is important to pay attention and ascertain what factors work as triggers for oneself.

TOOLS *and* TECHNIQUES

8. Enhancing Coherence, Resilience and Equanimity in One's Day-to-Day Life

Coherence implies a form of order or focus—*coherent thought* implies very focused, clear non-random thought as opposed to disorganized, haphazard, "noisy" thought processes that we are used to in our day-to-day living. Going from random incoherent thought to coherent consciousness can be as powerful as going from incandescent (incoherent) light to a laser beam, particularly given the holographic organization of the universe (holographic images can be created using laser light but cannot be created with incandescent light).

By achieving a highly focused level of awareness, individuals are able to tap into normally unconscious or latent abilities. Moreover, achieving specialized states of consciousness may allow the individual to access hierarchical levels of information *enfolded* within the structure of the C Field and as such, the universe itself.

As referenced earlier, access to the more universal information/intelligence aspects of the C Field (which is enhanced by increased coherence and guided by an individual's resonance—i.e., like attracts like on a thought/consciousness level) enhances creativity, vision and intuition; promotes key insights and discoveries;and facilitates higher understanding of anything and everything, including profound and not so profound spiritual matters.

Enhanced coherence can be accomplished via any of the various tools and techniques described above. There is considerable evidence to suggest that these various tools and techniques (and the Peak Experiences they can facilitate) can have major and lifelong effects that enhance one's capabilities as specifically delineated above and that more broadly enhance one's psychological, neurological and spiritual capabilities (see TOR Secondary Evidence #5).

It is also important to note that increasing one's coherence does not necessarily require accomplishing any particular "difficult" feat or austere lifestyle—or a specifically prescribed altered state of consciousness or OOBE such as those delineated in association with some of the tools and techniques described above.

In general, factors that increase one's resilience and equanimity also tend to increase one's coherence. Resilience is the capacity following adverse or stressful events to adapt to (and even thrive in) the resulting challenges and changing circumstances. Such a capacity proactively insulates and protects individuals from a variety of anxiety disorders and depression.

Similarly, *equanimity* is the inner strength and stability to experience well-being and confidence in the *eye of the storm*—enabling one to maintain a relaxed body and calm, balanced mind regardless of the circumstances. It allows one to remain centered and to see the big picture with perspective and patience.

Factors that are generally enjoyable for individuals that can increase one's resilience and equanimity include laughter, music, intimacy (including friendship and sexual intimacy), spiritual exploration and understanding, and sleep. Enhancing these factors can be a fun and compelling way to increase coherence while optimizing neurological function as well as psychological health (Ornish 1998, Wiebers 2001, Seligman 2002).

TWELVE KEY FACTORS FOR ENHANCING COHERENCE, RESILIENCE AND EQUANIMITY IN ONE'S DAY-TO-DAY LIFE

a. Develop a Balanced Worldview and Productive Attitude

Resilient people tend to view life's difficulties as challenges and respond accordingly with action rather than with fear, self-pity, blame or "victim mentality." While life can be very challenging, an important step in becoming more resilient is to develop positive "self-talk" to get away from the language of powerlessness and to remind yourself that you are strong and can get stronger and wiser as you handle life's challenges. If you feel that you have been wronged by someone, forgive them, move forward and own your experiences rather than being owned by them.

An example of the language of powerlessness is saying to yourself, "I have to take out the garbage" or "I have to take the kids to school." It is useful to realize that you don't have to do any of these things. Reflect on whether or not you are better off doing as opposed to not doing them and whether you really feel they are in your best interest and the best interest of others. Then engage in positive self-talk such as, "I want to take out the garbage" or "I want to take the kids to school."

b. Develop an Internal Locus of Control

Resilient people believe that they are in control of their lives, and while we can't control all of our circumstances or the actions of others, we can control how we respond to those circumstances and actions, and that makes a big difference in our attitudes and in the course that our lives take.

Anyone can develop and cultivate one's own internal locus of control under virtually any circumstance that life presents, including some of the worst circumstances that one can imagine. Such an internal locus greatly affects how people meet and deal with big challenges as well as day-to-day stresses.

Don't put off solving problems—inaction can reinforce the feeling that a problem is out of your control. Be decisive. Dismantle big problems into manageable small parts. Then, take on and solve these parts as a means to feel success and build confidence.

Recall how you met past challenges and use the same strategies to meet the stresses of today. By facing current problems with an eye to *solutions*, you are more likely to achieve a sense of progress and of "getting ahead" with life.

Resist the urge to blame others for your distress and don't blame yourself excessively.

c. Approach Life with Gratitude, Generosity and Compassion

Experiencing *gratitude* on a regular basis greatly enhances resilience and has been shown to have very beneficial effects on energy and enthusiasm. Gratitude is a positive emotion that occurs when you understand and acknowledge that the experiences you have in life, both large and small, are not owed to you but are gifts. It is the opposite of feelings of entitlement or taking things for granted.

You can increase your overall level of gratitude by increasing the number of people you feel grateful to in your life. Make it a point to write and then deliver a letter to someone who has been especially helpful or kind to you but has never been properly thanked.

You can also increase the number of circumstances you feel grateful for in your life. Take a week and, each evening, write down three things that went well that day and what caused them.

Generosity is the act of giving of oneself for the purpose of benefitting others. Cultivating generosity in one's life clearly enhances resilience and has been shown to have numerous psychological and other health benefits, including lower rates of depression and anxiety disorders, decreased chronic pain, decreased cardiovascular disease and increased life expectancy.

Selfless generosity is not to be confused with giving that is done with the motivation of manipulating or creating guilt in the receiver. Such "giving" is more properly identified as self-focused. It does not enhance resilience and has actually been shown to be harmful to the individual undertaking it.

Compassion is closely aligned with selfless giving and gratitude, involving kindness, caring and empathy for others along with the desire to help. It is among the highest of all forms of motivation for anything that we do.

Enhanced resilience, coherence and equanimity are correlated with extending the circle of one's compassion beyond oneself and one's immediate family to all humans (regardless of apparent external "differences" of nationality, race, economic class, religion, ethnicity, etc.) and also to all nonhuman beings and all life. Extending our circle of compassion is not only fundamental to our individual resilience, coherence and equanimity, but also to our evolution as individuals and as a species.

Perhaps the best antidote for personal fear or anxiety is to focus on caring for and worrying about how others are doing and being there to help them.

d. Cultivate Optimism

Being an optimist is more than looking on the bright side (though that helps). It's a way of viewing the world in which you maximize your strengths and accomplishments and minimize weaknesses and setbacks. It allows you to focus your attention and behavior on the opportunities and possibilities of life. Optimism does not involve a rose-colored lens but rather involves a clear lens, allowing you to see life realistically and clearly, without distortion. Developing a more optimistic worldview helps you to become more resilient.

In contrast, pessimism detracts from your resilience and acts as an internal stressor, creating a sense of threat (as opposed to opportunity and possibility) around the changes and challenges of life. Cultivating a more optimistic worldview involves practicing new beliefs and behaviors that are reflected in the choices you make in your day-to-day life.

Four Simple Things to Practice:
1. Focus on the positive, the opportunities and the possibilities throughout each day
2. Be *for* things, not *against* things
3. Laugh at yourself, not others
4. Resist the urge to complain

e. Know When to Be Assertive

Compassion, caring and selfless giving do not require acceding your control over your time or destiny to others, or automatically complying with the expectations or demands of others regarding your time, attention or resources. Indeed it is not desirable or psychologically healthy to do so. In these ways, *assertiveness* relates to your internal locus of control.

Ultimately, it is important for everyone to decide what is right for him- or herself. Yet, misconceptions about assertiveness commonly have a major adverse effect upon one's resilience.

For example, unreasonable concerns about looking selfish, feeling guilty or making someone irritated or angry can cause you to spend enormous amounts of time and energy engaging in unwanted activities with individuals or groups that are counterproductive or not a good match for what you feel you really need to do in life. Passive-aggressive or manipulative individuals may try to make you feel guilty or may become aggressive to try to control you. These situations create resilience problems for both the individual acceding control and those who are demanding it.

Setting limits with others and knowing when it is best for you to say "no" to requests, demands or invitations is probably the most effective thing that you can do to invoke a feeling of control over your life as you interact with others. Maintaining such control over one's time and destiny can be a critical factor for determining one's level of resilience, equanimity and coherence, and can account for enormous differences in one's effectiveness, creativity and success in accomplishing what is of personal importance in life.

f. Increase the Amount of Laughter in Your Life

If one is able to laugh at life's frustrations, one generally has much less vulnerability to stress and adversity. Those with a sense of humor about life tend to experience life as less stressful, are able to bond with others during difficult times, and enjoy numerous psychological and other health benefits.

Psychological benefits include enhanced resilience; prevention (and improvement) of anxiety disorders, depression and other psychiatric disorders; increased pain tolerance; stress reduction and enhanced general well-being. Other health benefits include enhanced immunity, improved blood pressure, and a reduction in cardiovascular disease and stroke.

Stepping back from a difficult situation long enough to maintain one's sense of humor provides perspective and increases one's resilience and equanimity almost immediately in that situation. Making laughter a major part of one's way of life has a broad impact on one's resilience, equanimity and coherence. Humor has also been shown to be a powerful tool for enhancing personal relationships and for almost instantaneously creating a more pleasant and enabling social environment.

People crave the uniquely enjoyable combination of physical, psychological and emotional feelings that laughter provides, and yet it is an activity that is obviously very good for one's health. Laughter is the antithesis of "heavy lifting" and creates a valuable win-win scenario for compelling enjoyment and enhanced health.

So enjoy more laughter in your life. Make it a point to set aside time to visit humorous websites or internet videos on a daily basis and share the best ones with friends who might enjoy them. Look for humor around you and spend more time with someone who really makes you laugh stridently and from your core. Watch a really funny movie or TV show at least once a week.

g. Involve Yourself in Music, the Arts and Other Forms of Creativity

Vibration is fundamental to everything in our universe. Sound vibrations in the form of music have been part of the human experience throughout recorded history and can play an important role in enhancing coherence, resilience and equanimity. Music can be a powerful communications vehicle which can generally reach more directly into the deeper parts of our consciousness than other forms of communication.

Music can have profound and almost instantaneous effects upon one's mood, can evoke long-forgotten memories, and can be inspirational, relaxing, healing and/or energizing depending upon its nature and one's level of coherence and frame of mind at any given point in time. It can play a key role in shifting one's awareness and accessing different levels of consciousness.

Both listening to and performing music can yield enormous psychological, emotional and health benefits. Creating one's own music can enhance one's creative abilities in other areas. Finding specific music and sounds that resonate deeply and inspire one's higher awareness can have a major impact on one's coherence and can facilitate PEs, OOBEs, CWOHS, ADC, PLR and other tools and techniques. Creating one's own music/sound tapes, CDs or other media that focus upon the sounds or forms of music that inspire, relax, heal and/or focus one's awareness can be a powerful way to enhance one's coherence.

Observing or participating in any other form of creative art can have similar effects upon an individual's coherence. The same principle applies—namely that of finding specific aspects of any of these art forms that deeply resonate with and inspire higher and more focused awareness.

Happily, these activities are often extremely compelling and fun while being good for one's health and enhancing one's overall psychological, neurological and spiritual capabilities.

h. Enhance Your Experiences of Love, Intimacy and Close Friendships

Intimacy and close friendships that are based upon loving relationships confer enormous psychological, emotional and health benefits. They also involve activities that are compelling and deeply fulfilling.

While human sexuality clearly offers one of the most intense forms of altered consciousness that one can naturally experience, it has also been stigmatized, distorted and repressed in so many ways by human society that it is often exceedingly difficult for individuals to unlock their own natural potential for highly ecstatic loving experiences.

It is clear that intense sexual intimacy and satisfaction, along with the increased fun and pleasure that accompany these, can add considerably to the depth of intimate relationships. Numerous techniques have been advanced that are based upon harnessing the energy associated with loving human sexuality and using it to enhance one's spiritual capabilities and resilience. On the other side of the spectrum, the fields of psychology and psychiatry both have entire divisions devoted to helping individuals with "sexual dysfunction" which is pervasive in our society.

To provide comprehensive advice on how to optimize one's sexual intimacy is beyond the scope of this book, but the following tips are often of fundamental importance:

1. Focus on the transcendent as well as the physical aspects of your activities.
2. Deeply recognize that you and your partner are completely worthy of a highly ecstatic experience.
3. Keep yourself in the present moment.
4. Drop your expectations, judgments, comparisons and your need to understand.
5. Surrender yourself.
6. Give all you have to give.
7. Receive all there is to receive.

Close friendships of all types can play an important role in determining how much we value ourselves and in our levels of resilience, equanimity and coherence. Entire books have been devoted to the subject of building friendships and nurturing them. Some recurrent themes that bear reflection in this arena are as follows:

1. Be a positive influence—bring optimism and humor to your friends.
2. Be supportive—offer help during trying times and difficult situations.
3. Drop the competitiveness and entitlements—friendships are not rivalries wherein one worries about who has the best job or

the smartest children, and one should not be tied to meeting one's own set of perceived entitlements.
4. Give of yourself in ways that are *mutually* fulfilling for you and your friends.
5. Celebrate accomplishments together.
6. Be sincere in your caring and in your attention.
7. Be good to yourself—you will be a much better friend if you love and care about yourself.

i. Get in Touch with Your Spiritual Side (Your Deeper Self)

Spiritual exploration is part of a journey that generally lasts throughout an individual's lifetime. As referenced above, from the time humans are born on this planet, they are taught to look outward and to look to various institutions—academic institutions, economic institutions, political institutions, social institutions, etc.—for meaning and for answers. In reality, they need to look inward for answers. Everything that is needed, including God (All That Is), is inward.

Self-realization and self-actualization substantively begin with exploring your deeper identity and with discovering the power of the real, "more authentic" you. Ultimately, this is fundamental to higher understanding, greater vision, increased creativity and greater effectiveness.

Meeting the real you and getting to *know* the real you (your real conscious self) is crucial as is coming to recognize that your body and brain and all the elements you "identify" with on this plane, such as your name and occupation, are mere vehicles and tools for temporarily expressing the real (and indestructible) you. The vehicles and tools generally add to the illusion of separation of yourself from the rest of the world around you. *Knowing* (as opposed to passively believing) the above is fundamental to virtually any form of what is referred to as spiritual enlightenment.

All of us have the capacity to explore, find and do all of this without undue dependence upon others or fear of taking one's own unique path. The key is coming to know the real you, the "inner" you, who is far more capable than the "other" you.

The exploration process and the very journey itself are of paramount importance in determining one's levels of coherence, resilience and equanimity.

j. Develop Your Optimal Program of Physical Exercise

Exercise has been shown to convey a variety of long- and short-term benefits to the brain and body. Regular physical exercise increases learning capacity, sharpens memory and boosts overall cognitive function. Exercise and physical fitness, particularly *aerobic fitness*, not only improve short-term mental processes but also decrease the long term risk of stroke, Alzheimer's disease and other forms of age-related cognitive decline.

Science has also associated regular exercise with improved sleep; improved self-esteem, mood and relaxation; improved bone density, with reduced risk of fractures; and decreased risk of obesity, cardiovascular disease, diabetes mellitus, hypertension and certain cancers.

Strength training has been associated with improved balance and coordination, better weight management, and greater strength and flexibility. *Overall activity level and NEAT (non-exercise activity thermogenesis)* are strongly associated with obesity and being overweight. Prolonged episodes of *physical inactivity* (sitting for periods of more than 1 hour throughout the day) is associated with risk for hypertension and diabetes mellitus independent of other measures of physical fitness.

Given the above benefits and risks, it is not surprising that optimal exercise and overall physical activity levels can have a strong impact on one's resilience, equanimity and coherence.

Five Key Exercise Components:
1. *Overall Activity Level*—parking one's car farther away from destinations, family walks, taking the stairs instead of elevators, playing family games, etc.
2. *Motion*—decreasing uninterrupted hours of sitting associated with screen time (computer and TV) and phone time
3. *Steps*—tracking steps with a pedometer
4. *Aerobic Exercise*—numerous options with varying intensities based upon personal interest and capabilities
5. *Strength Training*—8–10 exercises twice per week

When undertaking any exercise program, it is important to find activities that you enjoy that readily fit into your daily routine. Many of the five key exercise components above, particularly as they relate to the first three categories, can be simple and easy to do but can have enormous benefit over time. For other exercise activities or any health condition that may preclude exercise in any of its forms, it is wise to check with one's doctor prior to undertaking new activities.

Numerous studies have also documented that exercising with others— taking part in family exercise activities or group exercise classes, or having a training partner—can greatly improve your exercise adherence.

Exercising together as a family is a great way to strengthen family bonds and relationships. Good health and fitness make every day of life better and more fulfilling for parents and children alike. Children learn about exercise, proper nutrition, stress management and healthy living from what they see at home. When the family spends time engaged in physical activity, it is much easier for kids to stay healthy and adopt a lifelong healthy lifestyle.

Exercise classes are another great way to get more exercise, and the benefits of social exercise are clear: companionship, motivation, support, encouragement, friendship and fun. Safety is another reason for exercising with others, especially outdoors.

One of the best things you can do to get yourself to exercise is to get a partner. Find a friend to exercise with and make an agreement to get each other moving. Find a person who is in pretty much the same shape you are in so you can stay together. Research has shown that participants were calmer and more tired after exercising with another person. Exercising with another person also increases competition and therefore the rigor of the workout.

Having a regularly scheduled exercise time, at which others are depending on you, is an excellent way of ensuring that you maintain a high exercise adherence. If you have arranged to exercise with a training partner or as part of a family or group exercise, you are more likely to keep that appointment rather than miss it and let others down.

Target Exercise Goals:
1. *General Activity Level*—maintain an active lifestyle *and* maximize overall activity
2. *Motion*—minimize hours of uninterrupted sitting
3. *Steps*—10,000 steps per day
4. *Aerobic Exercise*—moderately intense activity for 30 minutes three to five times per week
5. *Strength Training*—8–10 exercises, 10–15 repetitions each twice per week

k. Choose Brain-Healthy Nutrition

Good food choices can enhance short-term brain function, emotional management and body function, and can preserve brain/body/emotional function and protect against disease and disability for the long-term. Antioxidants in plant foods, including fruits, vegetables, grains, seeds, and nuts, may counter damaging effects of free radicals on brain function.

The ideal and clean-burning fuel for the brain is *glucose*. The brain accounts for roughly 2% of body weight but consumes approximately 20–30% of our daily calories, relying primarily on a constant supply of glucose obtained from recently eaten carbohydrates (fruits, vegetables, grains, etc.).

Complex carbohydrates (fruits, vegetables, legumes, whole cereals and grains) are generally the most desirable brain foods as they take longer to break down into simple sugars and thereby provide a more *steady source of energy* which the brain prefers.

Under circumstances of deprivation, the brain will use protein and fat for fuel. *Protein* may be converted to glucose, but this also produces ammonia, a toxic byproduct which the body converts to less toxic urea, which the kidneys must clear from the body. *Fat* breakdown produces acetate and ketone bodies (not glucose), which can be used by some body tissues for fuel but which are not ideal fuels for the brain.

Numerous studies have documented that *diets rich in fruits, vegetables and whole grains, and low in saturated fat, cholesterol and added/refined sugar* can protect against stroke, Alzheimer's disease and other age-related cognitive decline. Science has also associated such diets with protective effects against cardiovascular disease, diabetes mellitus, hypertension, obesity and certain cancers (colon, breast, prostate).

Diets low in fruits, vegetables, whole grains and fiber, and high in saturated fat, cholesterol and added sugar are associated with increased risk of the above diseases/disorders, cognitive decline and long-term disability.

Optimizing brain function and overall health can have a major impact upon one's coherence, resilience and equanimity, as well as one's overall neurological and psychological capabilities.

Countless nutrition programs and diets have been developed and recommended over the years. Here is a simple but profound prescription for optimizing brain function and overall health which focuses on four things—maximizing two and minimizing the other two.

MAXIMIZE:
1. *Fruits and Vegetables*
2. *Fiber* (from healthy sources)—fruits, vegetables, whole grains and legumes

MINIMIZE:
3. *Cholesterol and Saturated Fat*—meat, dairy, eggs
4. *Three Main Sources of Excess Calories*—sugar-sweetened beverages, junk food, calorie-dense snacks

In establishing your own optimal eating habits, it is important to start wherever you are and take small steps to change any of the four components in the right direction. You can work on any or all of the four components, but it is generally best to start with one or two that are the easiest for one to change. As you get used to success, other changes will follow and become easier.

As with exercise, it is important to remember that small changes, even though they may be simple, can have a major impact, particularly over long periods of time. It is also important to note that getting yourself and your family into the right habits early in life can have a huge impact.

It is also important to keep in mind that food, like all physical matter, is fundamentally energy and vibration and is a manifestation of consciousness. This is particularly relevant in regard to the eating of nonhuman animals and animal products. Most of our meat and dairy products are a living, vibratory embodiment of cruelty, violence, enslavement and despair, and by consuming such products we take on whatever cruelty, violence, enslavement and despair is embodied within them. This can damage not only one's physical health but also one's emotional and spiritual health.

Note: If you believe that you or any of your family members may have an eating disorder (such as anorexia nervosa or bulimia), it is wise to check with your doctor to obtain personal medical advice.

l. Maintain Optimal Sleep Habits

Sleep is necessary for our nervous systems to work properly. Too little sleep leaves us drowsy and unable to concentrate the next day. It also leads to impaired memory and physical performance and reduced ability to carry out various calculations. If sleep deprivation continues, hallucinations and mood swings may develop. There are considerable individual differences in sleep duration (and presumably sleep requirements) across all ages, and the average duration and patterns of sleep changes with age.

With maturation, there are prominent changes in sleep structure (architecture), such as a decrease in the amount of REM (rapid eye movement) sleep from birth (50% of sleep) through early childhood into adulthood (25–30% of sleep). In addition, the initial preponderance of deep- or slow-wave sleep in early childhood decreases after puberty and continues to decline over one's lifespan. School-aged children (6–12 years of age) average approximately 10–11 hours of sleep in a 24-hour period. Research studies suggest that adolescents generally require about 9–9.25 hours of sleep per night; however, many are getting less than 8 hours of sleep per school night.

Adults average about 7–8 hours of sleep per day. Total sleep time, sleep efficiency, percentage of slow-wave sleep and percentage of REM sleep significantly decrease with age, while light sleep and waking after sleep onset increase with age. The decline in deep sleep begins around ages 35 to 50. However, it is important to note that these changes are less prominent among women and in the healthiest older adults.

The amount of sleep that you need is that optimum amount that allows you to function throughout the day without feeling drowsy when you sit quietly.

Activity in parts of the brain that control emotions, decision-making processes and social interactions is drastically reduced during deep sleep, suggesting that this type of sleep may help people maintain optimal emotional and social functioning while they are awake.

It is clear that optimizing one's sleep can have a major impact upon one's resilience, which in turn affects one's equanimity and coherence.

Attention to the following eight key sleep hygiene tips can have a great impact upon the quality and quantity of one's sleep.

Eight Key Sleep Hygiene Tips:

1. *Set a schedule*: Go to bed at a set time each night and get up at the same time each morning. Disrupting this schedule may lead to insomnia. Sleeping in on weekends also makes it harder to wake up early on Monday morning because it resets your sleep cycles for a later awakening.

2. *Relax before bed*: You can train yourself to associate certain restful activities with sleep and make them part of your bedtime ritual. Do the same things each night to tell your body it's time to wind down. This may include taking a warm bath or shower, reading a book or listening to soothing music. Relaxing activities done with lowered lights can help ease the transition between wakefulness and sleepiness. Conversely, sleep may be impeded by stimulating pursuits such as working, emailing, paying bills, watching TV, exercising or dealing with strong emotional issues.

3. *Go to bed when you're tired and don't lie in bed awake*: If you can't get to sleep, don't just lie in bed. Do something else, like reading, watching television or listening to music, until you feel tired. The anxiety of being unable to fall asleep can actually contribute to sleeplessness.

4. *Exercise*: Try to exercise for at least 20 to 30 minutes a day. Daily exercise, especially aerobic exercise, often helps people sleep. Note, however, that a workout soon before bedtime may interfere with sleep. For maximum benefit, try to get your exercise about 5 to 6 hours before going to bed.

5. *Avoid caffeine, nicotine and alcohol*: Avoid drinks that contain the stimulant caffeine for 8 hours prior to your planned bedtime. Sources of caffeine include coffee, chocolate, soft drinks, non-herbal teas, diet drugs and some pain relievers. Smokers tend to sleep very lightly and often wake up in the early morning due to nicotine withdrawal. Alcohol robs people of deep sleep and REM sleep and keeps them in the lighter stages of sleep.

6. *Don't eat or drink large amounts before bedtime*: Eat a light dinner at least 2 hours before sleeping. If you're prone to heartburn, avoid spicy or fatty foods, which can make your heartburn flare and prevent a restful sleep. Also, limit how much you drink before bed. Too much liquid can cause you to wake up repeatedly during the night for elimination trips.

7. *Sleep until sunlight*: If possible, wake up with the sun, or use very bright lights in the morning. Sunlight helps the body's internal biological clock reset itself each day. Sleep experts recommend exposure to an hour of morning sunlight for people having problems falling asleep.

8. *Control your room temperature and environment*: Maintain a comfortable temperature in the bedroom. Extreme temperatures may disrupt sleep or prevent you from falling asleep.

Create a room that's ideal for sleeping. Adjust the lighting, temperature, humidity and noise level to your preferences. Use blackout curtains, eye covers, earplugs, extra blankets, a fan or white-noise generator, a humidifier or other devices to create an environment that suits your needs.

Note: It is also important for you and your physician to recognize that a wide variety of health issues may disrupt your sleep, including pain, pregnancy, depression or illness—everything from a cold to a more serious disease. In addition, if you have a persistent sleeping problem wherein you have trouble falling asleep night after night, or you always feel tired the next day, then you may have a specific medical sleep disorder and should see a physician.

GLOSSARY *of* ABBREVIATIONS

ADC	After-Death Contact
C Field	Consciousness Field
C Unit	Consciousness Unit
CWOHS	Connecting with One's Higher Self
DMT	Dimethyltryptamine (a psychedelic drug)
EEG	Electroencephalography/Electroencephalogram
fMRI	Functional Magnetic Resonance Imaging
LSD	Lysergic acid diethylamide (a psychedelic drug)
MRI	Magnetic Resonance Imaging
NDE	Near-Death Experience
NEAT	Non-Exercise Activity Thermogenesis
OOB	Out-of-Body
OOBE	Out-of-Body Experience

PE	Peak Experience
PET	Positron Emission Tomography
PLR	Past-Life Recall/Regression
REM	Rapid Eye Movement
TOR	Theory of Reality
ZPE	Zero-Point Energy

TOR EVIDENCE CATEGORY REFERENCES

Acterberg J, Cooke K, Richards T, Kozak L, Lake J. Evidence for Correlations Between Distant Intentionality and Brain Function in Recipients: An fMRI Analysis. *Journal of Alternative and Complementary Medicine.* 2005; 11(6): 965–71.

Anderson MH, Ensher JR, Matthews MR, Wieman CE, Cornell EA. Observations of Bose-Einstein Condensates in a Dilute Atomic Vapor. *Science.* 1995; 269: 198–201.

Aspect A, Dalibard J, Roger G. Experimental Test of Bell's Inequalities Using Time-Varying Analyzers. *Physical Review Letters.* 1982; 49: 1804–7.

Backster C, White S. Biocommunications Capability: Human Donors and In Vitro Leukocytes. *International Journal of Biosocial Research.* 1985; 7: 132–46.

Barrow JD, Tipler FJ. *The Anthropic Cosmological Principle.* Oxford: Oxford University Press, 1986.

Beauregard M. Mind Really Does Matter: Evidence from Neuroimaging Studies of Emotional Self-Regulation, Psychotherapy, and Placebo Effect. *Progress in Neurobiology.* 2007; 81(4): 218–36.

Begley S. *Train Your Mind, Change Your Brain: How a New Science Reveals Our Extraordinary Potential to Transform Ourselves.* New York: Ballantine Books, 2007.

Berkovich SY. On the Information Processing Capabilities of the Brain: Shifting the Paradigm. *Nanobiology.* 1993; 2: 99–107.

Bernstein N. *The Co-ordination and Regulation of Movements.* Oxford: Pergamon Press, 1967.

Bishof M. Field Concepts and the Emergence of a Holistic Biophysics. In: Beloussov LV, Popp FA, Voeikov VL, Van Wijk R, Eds. *Biophotonics and Coherent Systems.* Moscow: Moscow University Press, 2000.

Blackmore S. Birth and the OBE: An Unhelpful Analogy. *Journal of the American Society for Psychical Research.* 1983; 77: 229–38.

Bohm D. *Coherence and the Implicate Order.* London: Routledge & Kegan Paul, 1980.

Bohm D, Hiley BJ. *The Undivided Universe: An Ontological Interpretation of Quantum Physics.* London/New York: Routledge, 1995.

Bouwmeester D, Pan JW, Mattle K, Eibl M, Weinfurter H, Zeilinger A. Experimental Quantum Teleportation. *Nature.* 1997; 390: 575–79.

Cahan D. *Hermann von Helmholtz and the Foundations of Nineteenth-Century Science.* Berkeley, CA: University of California Press, 1994.

Campbell FW, Robson JG. Applications of Fourier Analysis to the Visibility of Gratings. *Journal of Physiology.* 1968; 197: 551–66.

Carter C. *Science and the Near-Death Experience: How Consciousness Survives Death.* Rochester, VT: Inner Traditions, 2010.

Casimir HBG, Polder D. The Influence of Retardation on the London-van der Waals Forces. *Physical Review.* 1948; 73(4): 360–72.

Cavagna A, Cimarelli A, Giardina I, Parisi G, Santagati R, Stefanini F, Viale M. Scale-free Correlations in Starling Flocks. *Proceedings of the National Academy of Sciences.* 2010; 107(11): 865–70.

Chaneliere T, Matsukevich DN, Jenkins SD, Lan SY, Kennedy TAB, Kuzmich A. Storage and Retrieval of Single Photons Transmitted Between Remote Quantum Memories. *Nature.* 2005; 438: 833–36.

Danielson C. Report of Findings: Phase II of a Study on the Effects of Long-Term Participation in the Monroe Institute Programs. www.monroeinstitute.org: 2010.

Davis KB, Mewes M-O, Andrews MR, van Druten NJ, Durfee DS, Kurn DM, Ketterle W. Bose-Einstein Condensation in a Gas of Sodium Atoms. *Physical Review Letters.* 1995; 75: 3969–3973.

Del Giudice E, Doglia S, Milani M. Self-Focusing of Frohlich Waves and Cytoskeleton Dynamics. *Physics Letters.* 1982; 90A: 104–6.

Del Giudice E, Doglia S, Milani M, Vitiello G. A Quantum Field Theoretical Approach to the Collective Behavior of Biological Systems. *Nuclear Physics.* 1985; B251: 375–400.

DeValois KV, DeValois RL, Yund WW. Responses of the Striate Cortex Cells to Grating and Checkerboard Patterns. *Journal of Physiology.* 1979; 291: 483–505.

Dotta BT, Buckner CA, Lafrenie RM, Persinger MA. Photon Emissions from Human Brain and Cell Culture Exposed to Distally Rotating Magnetic Fields Shared by Separate Light-Stimulated Brains and Cells. *Brain Research.* 2011; 1388: 77–88.

Duane TD, Behrendt T. Extrasensory Electroencephalographic Induction Between Identical Twins. *Science.* 1965; 150(3694): 367.

Dürr H-P, Popp F-A, Schommers W, Eds. *What Is Life? Scientific Approaches and Philosophical Positions.* Singapore: World Scientific Publishing, 2002.

Einstein A, Podolsky B, Rosen N. Can Quantum-Mechanical Description of Physical Reality Be Considered Complete? *Physical Review.* 1935; 47: 777–80.

Einstein A. Physics and Reality. *The Journal of the Franklin Institute.* 1936; 221: 349–82.

Einstein A. *Ideas and Opinions.* New York: Three Rivers Press/Random House, 1995.

Engel GS, Calhoun TR, Read EL, Ahn T-K, Manal T, Cheng Y-C, Blankenship RE, Fleming GR. Evidence for Wavelike Energy Transfer Through Quantum Coherence in Photosynthetic Systems. *Nature.* 2007; 446: 782–86.

Feynman RP. *Quantum Electrodynamics.* Reading, MA: Addison Wesley, 1962.

Fröhlich H. Long-range Coherence and Energy Storage in Biological Systems. *International Journal of Quantum Chemistry.* 1968; II: 641–49.

Fröhlich H. General Theory of Coherent Excitations on Biological Systems. In: Adey WR, Lawrence AF, Eds: *Nonlinear Electrodynamics in Biological Systems.* New York: Plenum Press, 1984.

Fröhlich H. Coherent Excitations in Active Biological Systems. In: Gutman F, Keyzer H, Eds. *Modern Bioeletrochemistry,* New York: Springer, 1986.

Gazdag L. *Beyond the Theory of Relativity.* Budapest: Robottechnika Kft, 1998.

Greyson B. Near-Death Experiences and Personal Values. *American Journal of Psychiatry.* 1983; 140: 618–20.

Greyson B, Harris B. Clinical Approaches to the Near-Death Experience. *Journal of Near-Death Studies.* 1987; 6: 41–55.

Greyson B. Biological Aspects of Near-Death Experiences. *Perspectives in Biology and Medicine.* 1998; 42(1): 14–32.

Grundler W, Keilmann F. Sharp Resonances in Yeast Growth Proved Nonthermal Sensitivity to Microwaves. *Physical Review Letters.* 1983; 51: 1214–16.

Heisenberg W. *Physics and Beyond.* New York: Harper & Row, 1971.

Holdon JM, Greyson B, James D. *Handbook of Near-Death Experiences: Thirty Years of Investigation.* Santa Barbara, CA: ABC-CLIO, 2009.

Kafatos M, Nadeau R. *The Conscious Universe: Parts and Wholes in Modern Physical Theory.* New York: Springer-Verlag, 2000.

Lamoreaux SK. Demonstration of the Casimir Force in the 0.6 to 6 μm Range. *Physical Review Letters.* 1997; 78: 5–8.

Laszlo E. *The Connectivity Hypothesis: Foundations of an Integral Science of Quantum, Cosmos, Life and Consciousness.* Albany, NY: State University of New York Press, 2003.

Li KH. Coherence: A Bridge Between Micro- and Macro Systems. In: Belousov LV, Popp FA, Eds. *Biophotonics—Non-Equilibrium and Coherent Systems in Biology, Biophysics and Biotechnology.* Moscow: Bioinform Services, 1995.

Lommel P van. *Consciousness Beyond Life: The Science of the Near-Death Experience.* New York: HarperCollins, 2010.

Long J, Perry P. *Evidence of the Afterlife: The Science of Near-Death Experiences.* New York: HarperOne/HarperCollins, 2010.

Long WJ. *How Animals Talk: And Other Pleasant Studies of Birds and Beasts.* Rochester, VT: Bear & Co., 2005.

Lutz A, Dunne JP, Davidson RJ. Meditation and the Neuroscience of Consciousness: An Introduction. In: Zelazo DP, Moscovich M, Thompson E, Eds. *The Cambridge Handbook of Consciousness.* Cambridge, UK: Cambridge University Press, 2007.

Maslow AH. *Religions, Values and Peak-Experiences.* New York: Penguin/Arkana, 1994.

Matsukevich DN, Kuzmich A. Quantum State Transfer Between Matter and Light. *Science.* 2004; 306: 663–66.

McFarland D. *Oxford Companion to Animal Behavior.* Oxford: Oxford University Press, 1982.

Moody RA. *Life After Life.* London/Toronto/New York: Bantam Books, 1976.

Moody RA, Perry P. *Glimpses of Eternity: Sharing a Loved One's Passage from This Life to the Next.* New York: Guideposts, 2010.

Morse M. *Closer to the Light.* New York: Ivy Books, 1990.

Morse M, Perry P. *Transformed by the Light: The Powerful Effects of Near-Death Experiences on People's Lives.* New York: Villard/Random House, 1992.

Nichol L. *The Essential David Bohm.* New York: Routledge, 2003.

Ornish D. *Love and Survival: The Scientific Basis for the Healing Power of Intimacy.* New York: HarperCollins, 1998.

Pascual-Leone A, Amedi A, Fregni F, Mcrabet LB. The Plastic Human Brain Cortex. *Annual Reviews of Neuroscience.* 2005; 28: 380.

Penfield W. *The Excitable Cortex in Conscious Man.* Liverpool: Liverpool University Press, 1958.

Penfield W. *The Mystery of the Mind: A Critical Study of Consciousness and the Human Brain.* Princeton: Princeton University Press, 1975.

Penrose R. *The Emperor's New Mind: Concerning Computers, Minds, and the Laws of Physics.* Oxford/New York: Oxford University Press, 1989.

Penrose R. *Shadows of the Mind: A Search for the Missing Science of Consciousness.* Oxford/New York: Oxford University Press, 1994.

Peoc'h R. Telepathy Experiments With Rabbits. *Foundation Odier de Psycho-Physique Bulletin.* 1997; 3: 25–28.

Persinger MA, Koren SA, Lafreniere GF. A NeuroQuantological Approach to How Human Thought Might Affect the Universe. *NeuroQuantology.* 2008; 3: 262–71.

Persinger MA, Saroka KS, Lavallee CF, Booth JN, Hunter MD, Mulligan BP, Koren SA, Wu H-P, Gang N. Correlated Cerebral Events Between Physically and Sensory Isolated Pairs of Subjects Exposed to Yoked Circumcerebral Magnetic Fields. *Neuroscience Letters.* 2010; 486(3): 231–34.

Pizzi R, Fantasia A, Gelain F, Rossetti D, Vescovi A. Nonlocal Correlations Between Separated Neural Networks. In: Donkor E, Pirich AR, Brandt HE, Eds. *Quantum Information and Computation II (Proceedings of SPIE—The International Society for Optics and Photonics).* 2004; 5436: 107–17.

Planck M. *A Survey of Physical Theory.* New York: Dover Publications, 1993.

Pokorny J, Wu T-M. *Biophysical Aspects of Coherence and Biological Order.* New York: Springer, 1998.

Popp F-A, Beloussov LV. *Integrative Biophysics: Biophotonics.* Dordrecht, The Netherlands: Kluwer Academic Publishers, 2010.

Pribram K. *Languages of the Brain.* Monterey, CA: Wadsworth Publishing, 1977.

Prigogine I, Stengers I. *Order Out of Chaos: Man's New Dialogue with Nature.* Boulder, CO: New Science Press, 1984.

Puthoff H, Targ R. A Perceptual Channel for Information Transfer Over Kilometer Distances: Historical Perspectives and Recent Research. *Proceedings of the IEEE.* 1976; 64(3): 329–54.

Radin D. Event-related Electroencephalographic Correlations Between Isolated Human Subjects. *Journal of Alternative and Complementary Medicine.* 2004; 10(2): 315–23.

Richards TL, Kozak L, Johnson LC, Standish LJ. Replicable Functional Magnetic Resonance Imaging Evidence of Correlated Brain Signals Between Physically and Sensory Isolated Subjects. *Journal of Alternative and Complementary Medicine.* 2005; 11(6): 955–63.

Ring KA. *Heading Toward Omega: In Search of the Meaning of the Near-Death Experience.* New York: Quill/William Morrow, 1984.

Ring KA, Elsaesser-Valarino S. *Lessons from the Light: What We Can Learn from the Near-Death Experience*. New York/London: Insight Books/Plenum, 1998.

Ring KA, Cooper SA. *Mindsight: Near-Death and Out-of-Body Experiences in the Blind.* Bloomington, IN: iUniverse, 2008.

Romijn H. About the Origin of Consciousness: A New Multidisciplinary Perspective on the Relationship Between Brain and Mind. *Proceedings of the Koninklijke Nederlandse Akademie van Wetenschappen.* 1997; 100(1-2): 181–267.

Sabom M. *Recollections of Death.* New York: Harper & Row, 1982.

Schwartz JM, Begley S. *The Mind and the Brain: Neuroplasticity and the Power of Mental Force.* New York: Regan Books, 2002.

Seligman MEP. *Authentic Happiness: Using the New Positive Psychology to Realize Your Potential for Lasting Fulfillment.* New York: The Free Press, 2002.

Sheldrake R. *The Presence of the Past: Morphic Resonance and the Habits of Nature.* Rochester, VT: Park Street Press, 1995.

Sheldrake R, Lawlow C, Turney. Perceptive Pets: A Survey in London. *Biology Forum.* 1998; 91.

Sheldrake R. *Dogs That Know When Their Owners Are Coming Home: And Other Unexplained Powers of Animals.* New York: Three Rivers Press/Random House, 2011.

Sparnaay MJ. Measurements of Attractive Forces Between Flat Plates. *Physica.* 1958; 24(6-10): 751–64.

Standish LJ, Johnson LC, Kozak L, Richards T. Evidence of Correlated Functional Magnetic Resonance Imaging Signals Between Distant Human Brains. *Alternative Therapies in Health and Medicine.* 2003; 9(1): 128.

Standish LJ, Kozak L, Johnson LC, Richards T. Electroencephalographic Evidence of Correlated Event-Related Signals Between the Brain of Spatially and Sensory Isolated Subjects. *Journal of Alternative and Complementary Medicine.* 2004; 10(2): 307–14.

Stevenson I. *Twenty Cases Suggestive of Reincarnation.* Charlottesville, VA: University Press of Virginia, 1974.

Stevenson I. *Where Reincarnation and Biology Intersect.* Westport, CT: Praeger, 1997.

Targ R, Puthoff HA. Information Transmission Under Conditions of Sensory Shielding. *Nature*. 1974; 251: 602–7.

Vitiello G. *My Double Unveiled: The Dissipative Quantum Model of Brain (Advances in Consciousness Research)*. Philadelphia/Amsterdam: The John Benjamins Publishing Company, 2001.

Wackermann J, Seiter C, Keibel H, Walach H. Correlations Between Brain Electrical Activities of Two Spatially Separated Human Subjects. *Neuroscience Letters*. 2003; 336: 60–64.

Wheeler JA. *Geometrodynamics*. New York: Academic Press, 1962.

Wiebers DO. *Stroke-Free for Life: The Complete Guide to Stroke Prevention and Treatment*. New York: HarperCollins, 2001.

Wigner E. The Problem of Measurement. *Journal of Physics*. 1963; 31: 6.

Wilson, C. *Super Consciousness: The Quest for the Peak Experience*. London: Watkins, 2009.

Zbinden H, Brendel J, Gisin N, Tittel W. Experimental Test of Nonlocal Correlation in Relativistic Configurations. *Physical Review A*. 2001; 63(2): 022111: 1–10.

TOR TOOLS and TECHNIQUES REFERENCES

Buhlman W. *Adventures Beyond the Body: How to Experience Out-Of-Body Travel*. New York: HarperCollins, 1996.

Carter C. *Science and the Near-Death Experience: How Consciousness Survives Death*. Rochester, VT: Inner Traditions, 2010.

Chadwick G. *Discovering Your Past Lives*. Chicago: Contemporary Books, 1988.

Coit L. *Listening: How to Increase Awareness of Your Inner Guide*. Ventura, CA: Las Brisas Publishing, 2002.

Danielson C. Report of Findings: Phase II of a Study on the Effects of Long-Term Participation in the Monroe Institute Programs. www.monroeinstitute.org: 2010.

Freke T. *Encyclopedia of Spirituality*. New York: Sterling Publishing, 2000.

Gawain S. *Creative Visualization*. Novato, CA: New World Library, 2002.

Gee J. *Intuition: Awakening Your Inner Guide*. Newburyport, MA; Weiser Books, 1999.

Garfield P. *Creative Dreaming*. New York: Fireside, 1995.

Greyson B. Near-Death Experiences and Personal Values. *American Journal of Psychiatry*. 1983; 140: 618–20.

Greyson B, Harris B. Clinical Approaches to the Near-Death Experience. *Journal of Near-Death Studies.* 1987; 6: 41–55.

Greyson B. Biological Aspects of Near-Death Experiences. *Perspectives in Biology and Medicine.* 1998; 42(1): 14–32.

Gustus S. *Less Incomplete: A Guide to Experiencing the Human Condition Beyond the Physical Body.* Winchester, UK/Washington DC: O-Books/John Hunt Publishing, 2011.

Hadley J, Staudacher C. *Hypnosis for Change: A Practical Manual of Proven Hypnotic Techniques.* Oakland, CA: New Harbinger Publications, 1996.

Hewitt J. *The Complete Yoga.* New York: Random House, 1990.

Holdon JM, Greyson B, James D. *Handbook of Near-Death Experiences: Thirty Years of Investigation.* Santa Barbara, CA: ABC-CLIO, 2009.

LaBerge S. *Lucid Dreaming: A Concise Guide to Awakening in Your Dreams and in Your Life.* Boulder, CO: Sounds True, 2009.

Lommel P van. *Consciousness Beyond Life: The Science of the Near-Death Experience.* New York: HarperCollins, 2010.

Long J, Perry P. *Evidence of the Afterlife: The Science of Near-Death Experiences.* New York: HarperOne/HarperCollins, 2010.

Maslow AH. *Religions, Values and Peak-Experiences.* New York: Penguin/Arkana, 1994.

Monroe RA. *Journeys Out of the Body.* New York: Doubleday, 1971.

Monroe RA. *Far Journeys.* New York: Main Street Books/Doubleday, 1985.

Monroe RA. *Ultimate Journey.* New York: Doubleday, 1994.

Moody RA. *Life After Life.* London/Toronto/New York: Bantam Books, 1976.

Moody RA, Perry P. *Coming Back: A Psychiatrist Explores Past-Life Journeys.* New York: Bantam Books/Doubleday, 1990.

Moody RA, Perry P. *Reunions: Visionary Encounters with Departed Loved Ones.* New York: Ivy Books, 1993.

Moody RA, Perry P. *Glimpses of Eternity: Sharing a Loved One's Passage from This Life to the Next.* New York: Guideposts, 2010.

Morse M. *Closer to the Light.* New York: Ivy Books, 1990.

Morse M, Perry P. *Transformed by the Light: The Powerful Effects of Near-Death Experiences on People's Lives.* New York: Villard/Random House, 1992.

Ornish D. *Love and Survival: The Scientific Basis for the Healing Power of Intimacy.* New York: HarperCollins, 1998.

Ring KA. *Heading Toward Omega: In Search of the Meaning of the Near-Death Experience.* New York: Quill/William Morrow, 1984.

Ring KA, Elsaesser-Valarino S. *Lessons from the Light: What We Can Learn from the Near-Death Experience.* New York/London: Insight Books/Plenum, 1998.

Ring KA, Cooper SA. *Mindsight: Near-Death and Out-of-Body Experiences in the Blind.* Bloomington, IN: iUniverse, 2008.

Roche L. *Meditation Made Easy.* New York: HarperCollins, 1998.

Rogo SC. *Leaving the Body: A Complete Guide to Astral Projection: A step-by-step presentation of eight different systems of out-of-body travel.* Englewood Cliffs, NJ: Prentice-Hall, 1983.

Sabom M. *Recollections of Death.* New York: Harper & Row, 1982.

Seligman MEP. *Authentic Happiness: Using the New Positive Psychology to Realize Your Potential for Lasting Fulfillment.* New York: The Free Press, 2002.

Stack R. *Out-of-Body Adventures: 30 Days to the Most Exciting Experience of Your Life.* Chicago/New York: Contemporary Books, 1988.

Stevenson I. *Twenty Cases Suggestive of Reincarnation.* Charlottesville, VA: University Press of Virginia, 1974.

Stevenson I. *Where Reincarnation and Biology Intersect.* Westport, CT: Praeger, 1997.

Wiebers DO. *Stroke-Free for Life: The Complete Guide to Stroke Prevention and Treatment.* New York: HarperCollins, 2001.

Wilson, C. *Super Consciousness: The Quest for the Peak Experience.* London: Watkins, 2009.

INDEX

A

abbreviations, glossary of, 167–68
After-Death Contact (ADC)
    endorphins and, 34
    memories of birth and, 29
    music and, 154–55
    as Peak Experience, 10, 112
    psychedelic drugs and, 35
    seizures and, 32–33
    telepathic communication with the dead, 38, 114, 133, 135
    tools and techniques, 133–36
alcohol, 26, 165
All That Is (God or the Divine)
    Connecting with One's Higher Self and, 129
    intelligence of, 46
    inward journey to, 9, 157
    oneness with, 1, 8, 11, 19
    perceptions of, 18
    prayer and, 146
Alzheimer's disease, 158, 161
animals, communication with, 72
anoxia, 31–32, 35
anxiety disorders, 11, 80, 148, 151, 153
art, 10, 77, 142, 146, 155
Aspect, Alain, 48, 69–70, 85–86, 92
assertiveness, 152–53
assisting others, as part of a spiritual adventure, 4, 110
astronomical phenomena
    cosmic coherence of, 54
    "empty space" and, 97, 100
    intelligence of, 13, 46
    particle and wave aspects of, 92
    resonance or vibration in, 51
    See also universe

B

Backster, Cleve, 72
Beauregard, Mario, 43
Bernstein, Nikolai, 63–64
birth, memories of, 29–30
blindness, and NDEs, 4, 10, 28, 29, 31, 37, 86, 116
body
   "empty space" and, 98, 101
   holographic organization of, 62, 64, 66
   instantaneous intercellular communication, 53–54, 72–73, 74, 93, 94
   intelligence of, 45, 47
   nutrition, healthy, 160–63
   physical exercise, importance of, 158–60
   rewards of separating consciousness from, 143
   as temporary vehicle, 1–2, 3, 8, 117, 136, 139, 157
   See also brain; Out-of-Body Experiences (OOBEs); senses, physical
Bohm, David
   C Field and, 73, 75–76
   on explicate vs. implicate order, 84, 86
   on holographic organization, 61, 84–85
   on plasmas and electrons, 47–48
Bohr, Niels, 52
Bose-Einstein condensates, 53, 93
Bouwmeester, Dirk, 48–49

brain
   in definitions of consciousness, 15, 16
   "empty space" and, 98, 101
   as facilitating (vs. creating) consciousness, 3, 7–9, 41–44
   holographic organization of, 18, 61–66, 106
   information-processing speed, 54, 74
   intelligence outside, 45–50, 75
   limiting or filtering functions of, 17–18, 79, 127, 139
   NDEs and brain (in)activity, 4, 9–10, 16, 26, 28, 31, 32, 37–38, 114, 115–16
   neuroplasticity of, 43
   nutrition, brain-healthy, 160–63
   oxygen deficiency and, 31–32, 33–34, 35
   past-life experiences and, 39
   physical exercise as beneficial to, 158
   resonance of cell membranes, 55–56
   rewards of separating consciousness from, 143
   as temporary vehicle, 1–2, 3, 8, 117, 136, 139, 157
   as transducer of wave-form information, 8, 18, 63–64, 83–84, 85, 91–92

C

C Field. *See* Consciousness Field (C Field)

Index

C Units. *See* Consciousness Units (C Units)
caffeine, 122, 165
Campbell, Fergus, 63
cancer, 47, 158, 161
carbon dioxide poisoning, 33–34
cardiovascular disease, 151, 153, 158, 161
Casimir, Hendrik, 99, 100
centering, as part of a spiritual adventure, 4, 105–6
Chaneliere, Thierry, 55–56
charting, as part of a spiritual adventure, 4, 107
children
    NDEs among, 28
    past-life experiences among, 38–39, 137–38, 142
    physical exercise and, 159
    sleep and, 163
coherence
    benefits of increasing, 5, 80
    C Field and, 12, 74, 147
    cosmic, 54–55
    ease of increasing, 11, 79–80, 106, 148
    factors that enhance health and, 11, 80, 148, 149–66
    vs. incoherent thought, 10, 51, 105, 147
    instantaneous intercellular communication, 53–54, 72–73, 74, 93, 94
    laser (coherent) light, 10, 51, 57–60, 63, 105, 147
    OOBEs and, 127
    Peak Experiences and, 112
    scientific demonstration of, 51–56

communication with the dead. *See* After-Death Contact (ADC)
compassion, cultivating, 151
Connecting with One's Higher Self (CWOHS)
    music and, 154–55
    OOBEs and, 126, 140
    Peak Experiences and, 10, 78, 112
    tools and techniques, 129–31
    See also spiritual advancement or enlightenment
consciousness
    brain as facilitating (vs. creating), 3, 7–9, 41–44
    coherence and, 10–11, 127, 147
    definitions of, 15–16, 44
    dissociation and, 27
    matter's relationship to, 2, 5, 8–9, 16–17, 43, 70, 71, 85, 162
    music and, 154
    particle aspect of, 18, 50, 94
    past-life experiences and, 39, 138, 139
    research on, 8–9, 41–44, 71–72
    rewards of separating, from body and brain, 143
    sexual intimacy as altered state of, 155
    sleep states and, 15, 122, 163–64
    subatomic particle behavior and, 13, 20, 49–50, 76
    subconscious vs. conscious mind, 3, 8, 129
    unanswered scientific questions about, 1, 7, 17
    wave aspects of, 12, 17, 55, 70, 94

consciousness (*continued*)
    See also Consciousness Field (C Field); Consciousness Units (C Units)
Consciousness Field (C Field)
    as fabric of universe, 12, 16, 19, 69–76, 95
    holographic organization of, 12, 20, 61, 66, 73, 106
    memories and, 15, 16, 18, 74–75
    as nonlocal, 12, 13, 20, 78, 79, 94
    OOBEs and, 127
    overview of, 12–13
    Peak Experiences and, 78, 79
    resonance and, 12, 15, 18, 56, 73, 147
Consciousness Units (C Units), 11–13, 16, 18–19, 20, 49–50
contemplation and prayer, 10, 112, 146
Cornell, Eric, 52
cosmological constant, 101
creativity
    assertiveness and, 153
    C Field and, 12, 20, 78, 147–48
    charting one's journey and, 2, 5, 9, 107
    discovering and, 108
    equipping and, 106
    hypnagogic state and, 123
    OOBEs and, 126, 127
    Peak Experiences and, 10, 78, 79, 80, 111, 143, 146, 154–55
    Principle of Unity and, 19
    self-discovery and, 157
    spiritual techniques and, 145–46

D

dance movement, as wave forms, 63–64
De Broglie, Louis, 78
death
    fear of, 27, 81, 117, 125–26
    shared experiences of, 36
    See also After-Death Contact (ADC); Near-Death Experiences (NDEs)
déjà vu, 32, 63
depersonalization, 26–27
depression, 11, 32, 80, 148, 153, 166
DeValois, Russell and Karen, 63, 85
diabetes mellitus, 158, 161
discovering, as part of a spiritual adventure, 4, 108–9
dissociation, 27
Divine, the. *See* All That Is (God or the Divine)
DMT (dimethyltryptamine), 35
Dotta, Blake, 73
dreams
    After-Death Contact vs., 135
    of blind people, 28, 29, 37, 116
    lucid dreams or dream control, 10, 112, 123, 145
    NDEs vs., 29
drugs, 26, 30–31, 34–35, 165

E

eating disorders, 163
ecstatic experiences, 155–56
EEGs. *See* electroencephalography (EEG)
Einstein, Albert
    on "empty space," 97, 99

on energy and matter's inseparability, 48, 69
on leaps in consciousness, 10, 78, 108
on pursuit of knowledge, 82
on quantum entanglement, 49, 52
electroencephalography (EEG)
consciousness research and, 42, 71–72
NDEs and, 4, 10, 32, 37, 115–16
particle aspect of consciousness and, 18, 94
"empty space," 97–102
endorphins, 31–32, 34
Engel, Gregory, 55
enlightenment. *See* spiritual advancement or enlightenment
entanglement
C Field and, 69–70, 71–73
coherence and, 52, 72, 73
higher-frequency dimensions and, 85–86
intelligence and, 48–49
nonlocal space and, 71, 84, 92
resonance and, 55
equanimity
coherence linked to, 5, 11, 80, 148
defined, 11, 80, 148
equipping and, 106
factors that enhance health and, 148, 149–66
Peak Experiences and, 112
equipping, as part of a spiritual adventure, 4, 106–7
evidence for Theory of Reality
on ability to exist without the brain, 37–39
on brain activity not being source of consciousness, 41–44
on C Field as a matrix underlying reality, 69–76
on coexistence of particle and wave aspects, 89–95
on coherence and resonance, 51–56
on dimensions at higher frequencies, 83–87
on holographic organization of brain and universe, 57–67
on intelligence outside the brain, 45–50
on NDEs' validity, 25–36
overview of evidence categories, 21–24
on Peak Experiences, 77–82
on vast energy in "empty space," 97–102
exercise, physical, 158–60, 164, 165

F

Feynman, Richard, 99
Fourier, Jean B. J., 63
Fourier analysis, 63–64, 65, 85, 91
free will, 9, 17, 43
friendship, 11, 80, 148, 155–57, 160
Fröhlich, Herbert, 93
functional magnetic resonance imaging (fMRI), 18, 42, 43, 66, 71–72

G

Gabor, Dennis, 57, 61
Gazdag, Laszlo, 73

generosity, cultivating, 150–51
Gisin, Nicolas, 49
glossary of abbreviations, 167–68
God. *See* All That Is (God or the Divine)
gratitude, cultivating, 150

H

hallucinations
    endorphins and, 32
    ketamine and, 34
    NDEs vs., 4, 9, 26, 30, 32, 37
    sleep deprivation and, 163
health
    compassion as beneficial to, 151
    exercise and, 158–60, 164, 165
    factors that enhance coherence and, 11, 80, 148, 149–66
    friendship as beneficial to, 11, 80, 148, 155–57, 160
    generosity as beneficial to, 150–51
    gratitude as beneficial to, 150
    hypnosis as tool for, 146
    laughter as beneficial to, 153–54
    music as beneficial to, 154
    nutrition and, 160–63
    optimism as beneficial to, 151–52
    sexual intimacy as beneficial to, 155
    sleep hygiene, 163–66
    yoga as beneficial to, 144
Helmholtz, Hermann von, 63
holograms and holographic principles
    brain as organized holographically, 18, 61–66, 106
    C Field as organized holographically, 12, 20, 61, 66, 73, 106
    laser (coherent) light and, 10, 51, 57–60, 63, 105, 147
    overview of, 57–61
    universe as organized holographically, 8, 10–11, 19, 60–61, 66–67, 84–85, 105–6, 147
human body. *See* body
human brain. *See* brain
humor. *See* laughter
hypercarbia, 33–34
hypnagogia, 122–23
hypnosis, 10, 112, 138–39, 142, 145–46
hypoxia, 31–32, 35

I

identity
    NDEs and, 26–27, 30, 31, 117
    as transcending body and brain, 1–2, 3, 8, 117, 136, 139, 157
    See also Connecting with One's Higher Self (CWOHS)
intelligence
    C Field and, 12, 19–20, 73–75
    at quantum level, 47–50
    of systems, 13, 45–47, 93
internal locus of control, 149–50, 152
intimacy. *See* friendship; sexual intimacy
intuition
    C Field and, 148

Connecting with One's Higher
    Self and, 131
discovery and, 108, 109
Einstein on, 10, 78, 108
as NDE benefit, 82, 117
PLR techniques and, 141
visualization and, 145

J

journal keeping, 109
Journeys Out of the Body (Monroe),
    119–20

K

ketamine, 34–35
Ketterle, Wolfgang, 52
knowledge, universal, 75, 78–79,
    126, 127, 130

L

LaBerge, Stephen, 145
Lamoreaux, Steve, 100
laser (coherent) light, 10, 51, 57–60,
    63, 105, 147
Laszlo, Ervin, 73
laughter, 11, 80, 148, 153–54
life reviews
    brain (in)activity and, 38
    C Field's memory storage and,
        16, 74–75
    endorphins and, 34
    holographic features of, 65–66
    memories of birth and, 29
    among NDE features, 114
    oxygen deficiency and, 32
    psychedelic drugs and, 35
    seizures and, 33
    unbiased nature of, 116–17
light, visions or beings of
    brain (in)activity and, 38
    Connecting with One's Higher
        Self and, 130, 131
    endorphins and, 34
    higher-frequency dimensions
        and, 86
    hypercarbia and, 33
    memories of birth and, 29
    among NDE features, 114
    psychedelic drugs and, 35
LSD (lysergic acid diethylamide), 35
lucid dreams, 10, 112, 123, 145

M

magnetic resonance imaging (MRI)
    consciousness research and, 42,
        43, 71–72
    holographic principles and,
        66–67
    particle aspect of consciousness
        and, 18, 94
    resonance and, 52
Maslow, Abraham, 77, 111
Matsukevich, Dzmitry, 55–56
matter
    consciousness's relationship to,
        2, 5, 8–9, 16–17, 43, 70, 71,
        85, 162
    Einstein on energy and, 48, 69
    "empty space" and, 97–102
    historical record of, 73
    illusionary nature of material
        world, 86
    particle and wave aspects of, 75,
        84, 89–95
    thought as resonant with, 55

meditation
　Connecting with One's Higher Self and, 129
　contemplation/prayer as, 146
　overview of, 144
　Peak Experiences and, 10, 78, 112
　visualization as, 145
memory
　of birth, 29–30
　brain anatomy and, 42, 44, 61–62
　C Field and, 15, 16, 18, 74–75
　holographic organization of, 61–63, 65, 106
　hypercarbia and, 33
　music and, 154
　NDEs' enhancement of, 27, 30, 31, 32, 38, 115
　nonlocal space and, 18, 39, 65, 75, 91, 138
　physical exercise as beneficial to, 158
　sleep deprivation and, 163
　See also Past-Life Recall/Regression (PLR)
mescaline, 35
metaphysical science, 1, 7
mirror gazing, 134
Monroe, Robert, 87, 119–20
Monroe Institute, 82, 126
Moody, Raymond, 134, 138–39
motivations, higher vs. lower, 105, 107, 109, 110, 116, 151
MRI. *See* magnetic resonance imaging (MRI)
music
　coherence/resilience/equanimity enhanced by, 11, 80, 148, 154–55
　hypercarbia and, 33
　during NDEs, 32, 114
　OOBEs and, 121, 154–55
　past-life memories of, 142
　Peak Experiences and, 10, 146, 154–55
　resonance and, 52
　sleep and, 164, 165
mysticism, 86–87

N

navigating, as part of a spiritual adventure, 4, 107–8
Near-Death Experiences (NDEs)
　access to universal knowledge in, 75, 78–79
　alternative explanations, overview of, 25
　blindness and, 4, 10, 28, 29, 31, 37, 86, 116
　brain (in)activity and, 4, 9–10, 16, 26, 28, 31, 32, 37–38, 114, 115–16
　Connecting with One's Higher Self and, 131
　features, overview of, 114
　Moody as early pioneer in, 134
　neurophysiological explanations, refuted, 31–36
　as Peak Experience, 10, 78, 81–82, 112
　psychological explanations, refuted, 26–31
　vs. shared death experiences, 36
　spiritual benefits of, 10, 26, 28, 30, 31, 38, 79, 81–82, 117–18
　tools and techniques, 113–18
　tunnel experiences, 29, 32, 33, 114, 140

See also life reviews; light, visions or beings of
NEAT (non-exercise activity thermogenesis), 158
neuroplasticity, 43
neuroscience
    consciousness as defined in, 15–16, 44
    consciousness research, 8–9, 41–44, 71–72
    instantaneous intercellular communication and, 53
    materialistic measuring techniques, 94
    memory research, 42, 44, 61–62
    need for new paradigms in, 14
    neurophysiological explanations for NDEs, 31–36
    TOR and, 1, 7
    See also brain; science
nicotine, 165
nonlocal space
    consciousness/C Field as, 12, 13, 20, 78, 79, 94
    entanglement and, 71, 84, 92
    memory storage and, 18, 39, 65, 75, 91, 138
    subatomic particle behavior and, 13, 20, 76, 84, 89
    timeless states and, 75, 78–79, 86, 87, 126, 139
nutrition, healthy, 160–63

O

obesity, 158, 161
optimism, cultivating, 151–52
Out-of-Body Experiences (OOBEs)
    After-Death Contact and, 134
    blindness and, 4, 10, 28, 37, 116
    breakdown of body image and, 31
    Connecting with One's Higher Self and, 129, 130
    depersonalization and, 27
    endorphins and, 34
    hallucinations and, 26
    memories of birth and, 29
    music and, 121, 154–55
    among NDE features, 114
    oxygen deficiency and, 32, 33
    as Peak Experience, 10, 78, 112, 119, 127
    PLR techniques and, 140
    psychedelic drugs and, 35
    tools and techniques, 87, 119–27
oxygen deficiency, 31–32, 33–34, 35

P

particle aspects
    coexistence of wave and, 75, 84, 89–95
    of consciousness, 18, 50, 94
    manifestations of, 12, 17, 69, 84, 94
Past-Life Recall/Regression (PLR)
    music and, 154–55
    as Peak Experience, 10, 112
    research on, 38–39, 137–38
    tools and techniques, 137–42, 145
Peak Experiences (PEs)
    access to universal knowledge in, 75, 78–79
    coherence linked to, 80, 148, 154–55
    feelings during, 4, 10, 77, 111

Peak Experiences (PEs) (*continued*)
  higher-frequency dimensions and, 87
  OOBEs as, 10, 78, 112, 119, 127
  phenomena and techniques, overview of, 10, 77–78, 111–12, 143–46
  research on, 81–82
  spiritual adventures and, 105, 106, 109
  triggers or facilitators for, 77, 146
Penfield, Wilder, 41–42
Penrose, Roger, 54–55
Perry, Paul, 134
Persinger, Michael, 55
personal identity. *See* identity
PET scans, 42, 43, 94
physics
  C Field and, 70, 75
  coherence and resonance in, 51–56
  on consciousness and matter, 9, 17, 43
  on energy density at higher frequencies, 83, 97–102
  need for new paradigms in, 14
  Nobel Prize in, 52, 57, 78, 99
  TOR and, 1, 7
  See also holograms and holographic principles; quantum physics
Planck, Max, 71, 97
Planck length, 99
Plato, 86
positron emission tomography (PET), 42, 43, 94
powerlessness, language of, 149
prayer, 10, 112, 146
precognition, 81, 117

pregnancy, 166
Pribram, Karl, 61, 74
Prigogine, Ilya, 93
psilocybin, 35
psychedelic drugs, 35
psychiatric disorders
  generosity as protecting against, 151
  laughter as protecting against, 153
  NDEs dismissed as, 26–29, 32
  resilience as protecting against, 11, 80, 148
  sleep disruptions and, 166

Q

quantum physics
  acceptance of wave-particle duality in, 75, 89–90
  applications to biology, 71–72, 93
  Bohm's achievements in, 84
  consciousness and subatomic particle behavior, 13, 20, 49–50, 76
  intelligence at quantum level, 47–50
  macroscopic phenomena, 52–53, 71
  Planck as founder of, 71, 97
  space as quantum vacuum, 98
  See also entanglement

R

reincarnation, 38–39, 137–38, 139
religion
  NDEs and religious affiliation, 27, 29, 81, 113, 117

OOBEs and, 119
Peak Experiences and, 78
prayer and, 146
yoga and, 144
REM (rapid eye movement) sleep, 163, 165
resilience
    coherence linked to, 5, 11, 80, 148
    defined, 11, 80, 148
    equipping and, 106
    factors that enhance health and, 148, 149–66
    Peak Experiences and, 112
resonance
    C Field and, 12, 15, 18, 56, 73, 147
    past-life experiences and, 39
    scientific demonstration of, 51–56
Reunions: Visionary Encounters with Departed Loved Ones (Moody, Perry), 134
Ring, Kenneth, 34–35

S

Schrödinger, Erwin, 52
science
    applications of quantum physics to biology, 71–72, 93
    brain as materialistic machine in, 9, 43
    coherence and resonance in, 51–56
    information aspect of C Field and, 73–74
    meeting of spirituality and, 13–14
    NDEs and materialistic approach to, 25, 36, 115, 116
    OOBEs and materialistic approach to, 87, 126
    Peak Experiences and materialistic approach to, 81
    PLR research, 38–39, 137–38
    unanswered questions in, 1, 7, 17
    unlocking secret of ZPE, 101
    See also neuroscience; physics; quantum physics; *and specific scientific authors and concepts*
seizures, 4, 9, 32–33, 37, 42
self. *See* identity
senses, physical
    blindness, and NDEs, 4, 10, 28, 29, 31, 37, 86, 116
    C Field and, 70, 75
    hallucinations and, 26
    holographic organization of, 62–63, 64, 65
    intelligence and, 47
    NDE reports and, 28, 31, 38, 115
    past-life sensory memories, 142
    reality as perceived by, 4, 8, 61
    wave aspects imperceptible to, 91, 92, 102
sexual intimacy, 11, 80, 148, 155–56
shared death experiences, 36
sharing, as part of a spiritual adventure, 4, 109–10
sleep
    coherence/resilience/equanimity enhanced by, 11, 80, 148
    consciousness and states of, 15, 122, 163–64
    hygiene, 163–66
    OOBE techniques and, 121–23, 125
    physical exercise as beneficial to, 158
    See also dreams

space-time
- brain's construction of, 17–18, 91–92
- entanglement and, 48–49, 52, 69–70, 71–72, 85–86, 92
- multiple dimensions in, 12–13, 20, 83–87
- timeless states, 75, 78–79, 86, 87, 126, 139
- *See also* nonlocal space

Sparnaay, M. J., 99, 100

Spinoza, Benedictus de, 86

spiritual advancement or enlightenment
- as active (vs. passive) process, 2, 5, 8, 9, 82, 103–4, 127, 157
- After-Death Contact and, 135
- coherence/resilience/equanimity linked to, 11, 80, 148, 157–58
- Connecting with One's Higher Self and, 131
- meat/dairy consumption and, 162–63
- meeting of science and spirituality, 13–14
- NDEs and, 10, 26, 28, 30, 31, 34, 38, 79, 81–82, 117–18
- OOBEs and, 125–27
- recognizing transience of body as key to, 2, 8, 117, 157
- sexual intimacy and, 155
- techniques, overview of, 10, 77–78, 111–12, 143–46

spiritual adventures, eight components of, 4, 103–10

Stevenson, Ian, 38–39, 137–38

stress
- endorphins and, 34
- internal locus of control and, 150
- laughter as protecting against, 153
- pessimism and, 152
- resilience and, 11, 80, 148

stroke, 153, 158, 161

subconscious mind
- capabilities of, vs. conscious mind, 3, 8, 129
- coherence and, 79
- as guiding choice of techniques, 106–7, 112
- PLR techniques and, 139, 140
- wave-based phenomena and, 8, 94

Surat Shabd Yoga, 145

T

T'ai Chi, 144

telepathy
- communicating with the dead via, 38, 114, 133, 135
- Connecting with One's Higher Self and, 131
- endorphins and, 34
- as enhanced intuitive capability of NDEs, 82, 117
- higher-frequency dimensions and, 86, 87
- OOBEs and, 126
- PLR techniques and, 140

Theory of Reality (TOR)
- condensed messages, 3–5
- consciousness paradigm, 15–20

evidence categories, overview of, 21–24
overview of, 1–2
three major components of, 1, 7–14
See also evidence for Theory of Reality; tools and techniques
thought balls, 10, 77, 78, 111, 131
time. *See* space-time
tools and techniques
    for After-Death Contact, 133–36
    for Connecting with One's Higher Self, 129–31
    for daily health, 149–66
    for NDEs, 113–18
    for OOBEs, 87, 119–27
    for Past-Life Recall/Regression, 137–42
    for Peak Experiences, 10, 77–78, 111–12, 143–46
tunnel experiences, 29, 32, 33, 114, 140

U

understanding, as part of a spiritual adventure, 4, 104–5
Unity, Principle of, 19
universe
    access to universal knowledge, 75, 78–79, 126, 127, 130
    C Field as fabric of, 12, 16, 19, 69–76, 95
    C Units as building blocks of, 11–13, 16, 18–19, 20
    connectedness with, 144
    cosmic coherence, 54–55
    "empty space" in, 97–102
    holographic organization of, 8, 10–11, 19, 60–61, 66–67, 84–85, 105–6, 147
    intelligence of, 13, 46, 50
    resonance or vibration in, 51, 73, 154
    unanswered scientific questions about, 1, 7
    as unified living process, 2, 5, 13, 50, 66, 85

V

victim mentality, 149
visualization
    Connecting with One's Higher Self and, 129
    goals of, 145
    OOBE techniques and, 121, 123, 124–25
    Peak Experiences and, 10, 112
    Principle of Unity and, 19
Vitiello, Giuseppe, 93

W

wave aspects
    brain as transducer of waveform information, 8, 18, 63–64, 83–84, 85, 91–92
    coexistence of particle and, 75, 84, 89–95
    of consciousness, 12, 17, 55, 70, 94
    of photons, as resonant, 55, 56

wave functions
  C Field and, 18, 73, 75–76, 95
  invisibility of, 92–93
  macroscopic, in organisms, 53, 94
Wheeler, John, 99–100
Wieman, Carl, 52
Wilson, Colin, 77, 111

Y

yoga, 10, 78, 112, 129, 144–45
Young, Thomas, 90

Z

zero-point energy (ZPE), 99, 101

ABOUT *the* AUTHOR

Dr. Wiebers is Emeritus Professor of Neurology at Mayo Clinic in Rochester, Minnesota. He has authored more than 340 scientific publications, five medical textbooks and two books for the general public. He lectures worldwide on medical and scientific topics and has been the recipient of numerous US and international awards for scientific and medical achievement. He has also served on the boards of eight national and international charitable organizations.

ABOUT TOR GROUP

TOR Group was formed in 2012 by David O. Wiebers, MD and colleagues, to change human thought about the nature of consciousness and the nature of reality and to empower people with new knowledge and practical tools that deepen their understanding of their conscious selves, their journey and their place in the universe. TOR Group strives to serve the greater good of individuals and society throughout the world by advancing the kinds of research, education, and service that support people's efforts to discover their essential selves and to advance their learning, creativity and human development.

For more information, visit:
torgroup.org.
Connect with TOR at
facebook.com/torgroup and twitter.com/torgroup.

ABOUT TOR FOUNDATION

TOR Foundation is a private, not-for-profit 501(c)(3) organization. It was formed in 2012 to provide education to the general public, scientific and medical communities and to provide financial support in the form of grants and special services contracts to organizations and endeavors that advance the TOR Group's message and strategic intent. TOR Foundation is funded on an annual basis by contributions from its affiliated organization, TOR Group, and by private donations.

For more information, visit:
torgroup.org.
Connect with TOR at
facebook.com/torgroup and twitter.com/torgroup.